A NEW BEGINNING TO OUR STORY

Erin Broek
A New Beginning to Our Story

Published by BooxAi
ISBN: 978-965-578-322-3

A NEW BEGINNING TO OUR STORY

A HEALTHY, PLANTED WOMAN WHO ABIDES
IN GOD

PEACE IN YOUR POSTPARTUM DEPRESSION

ERIN BROEK

CONTENTS

<u>To the moms:</u> You are not alone in your struggle with postpartum depression. Giving birth is a beautiful moment; seeing your child for the first time, who was just in your tummy rolling around and giving you kicks, letting you know they hear you. But because of the fall that happened in the garden between Adam and Eve, giving birth is a wake-up call and is traumatizing "to" your body and your mind. Through the dark nights thinking you are all alone, God was there. He was preparing your future for you. He was giving you the tools you needed to become a healthy, planted mom who abides in God instead of your depression. I pray this book will give you hope and understanding of your new journey with Christ.

<u>To my husband:</u> Thank you for being patient with me when I was struggling as a new mom. Thank you for helping me see that I needed to be nourished in Jesus. You gave me the strength that I need to get help and wake up from my depression. Your love for our daughter helped me to see that this is how Christ loves me.

<u>To my therapist:</u> You know who you are. I thank you for helping me with my trauma and giving me the tools to help me see the light of Jesus. You helped me wake up from my depression, and I thank you so much. You helped me set boundaries when spiritual warfare was at my door. And you were always there for me when I needed help, no question asked. Your voice, your oils, your pillows, your couch, your prayers, and just listening to me helped me become a stronger woman. I will never forget your kindness and your godly wisdom. May God give you strength in this time of need for

therapy. Now I can say back to you what gave me the strength to keep going (good job Erin!). Good job, therapist!

PREFACE

"Depression, fear, and anger is not our story, but peace, freedom, and joy is because of the blood of Jesus Christ."
~Erin Broek~

When you spend time alone, your mind goes like a fast train around and around the tracks. You think about everything you have done that day and what you should have done for the day. The whispers of the lies creep in, telling you that you are worthless and not strong enough. You start leaning in, listening instead of turning away. You start believing these truths. Your mind, once beautiful and innocent, starts becoming crippled by fear. You don't know what is right from wrong. You don't know how you got here. You can't even go outside because fear got you right where it wanted you. You start sleeping less, gaining more weight than you should, and you become an irritating person to be around. How did I let myself get here? How long have I been like this? Then, you start waking up and seeing these lies don't apply to you at all. You start speaking truth and encouraging words to yourself. You say to yourself, "You are beautiful, you are strong, you are brave, and you are a daughter of the Lord."

You see that what your pastors have been preaching to you every Sunday is what your soul needs to grow and to be healthy. You need to abide by God to reach your destination to become a well-rounded, healthy individual. You see around you now clearly. You can't believe you let yourself stoop so low that you completely lost your true self. You tell yourself you will be okay, but you know deep down that you are not okay. You tell yourself enough is enough. You need Jesus. You need His word. You need help. So, you nervously tell your husband, a friend, and a professional therapist that you are suffering from post-partum depression. You peel back the layers you have been holding onto so closely because they were your only hope. Well, you thought so. When you are sharing this sensitive information about yourself, you can breathe for the first time in months. You feel alive and ecstatic.

The dark depression cloud is erased by the beautiful rainbow of God's promises that He made to you and to all His people. You see now that Jesus was there even when you couldn't. You pray for the first time in months. You close your eyes and breathe in His grace and breathe out the fear you have been holding on to. You feel so close to God at this very moment. You let go of your depression and surrender it at your Messiah's feet. After praying, you see that your soul is dry and that you need to fall in love again with your Lord and Savior. So, you get your Bible from off your shelf and blow on it to get the dust off. You begin reading God's promises, and these beautiful words are like water that soothes your parched, sore throat. You see now that you can have a new beginning to your story because the Holy Spirit opened your eyes to see that you need change. You want help, you want to become healthy, and you want to abide in God.

If this story is similar to yours, then welcome, dear friend. Jesus loves you. This I know. Come and drink His everlasting love that will fill you with so much joy, peace, and understanding. Come as we begin to learn about our new story in Jesus. Jesus and His love story (the Bible) will help us become well-planted individuals. Yes, we can rest at His feet and listen, but we do need to do some gardening to get rid of some thorns and weeds that are planted in us. Jesus will give us "the nourishing, well rich soil" that will help us see that we are loved and beautiful in His sight. By God's grace and help, we will become healthy, well-rounded individuals. We cannot do this journey on our own. There is Jesus to help guide us and to give us the correct layout to show us how to grow our healthy gardens. Ladies get ready. Grab your shovels, your gloves, and your buckets. It's time to get dirty in beautiful truths by the gardener Jesus. And be watered by His everlasting love. Come with me as we abide in God together. Your friend,

Erin Cathleen Broek

~Breathe in God's Grace. Breathe out the Fear.~

Erin Broek

INTRODUCTION

A Garden Won't Produce if There Is No Nurturing
"Breathe in God's grace. Breathe out the Fear."
~Erin Broek~

Being home with my husband and child, I sit there glaring at my loved ones. I feel like a dark cloud is over my head, blocking my vision from seeing how wonderful God has blessed me. As a mom, I get angry at the littlest cries, laughter, and sounds. I sit there with a frown on my face and my arms crossed. I heard my husband say, "I love you, Erin," but it was like a whisper down the hall. My little girl reaches her hands out to me to be held, but I look at her with anger because she ruined my body. Haven doesn't even know how her birth caused so much pain in my body. I yell at Haven and say, "I have post-partum depression because of you, Haven!" I don't even see how hurtful those words are to my precious little angel. I think no one loves me or understands the trauma I went through having our baby girl. Why are my husband and daughter having such a joyful time when I am lost in despair? Time seems to keep slipping away. I sit in my house, scared out of my mind. I eat when I am not hungry because food feels like the only friend I have. I feel so lonely and sad all the time.

But then, I hear a beautiful bird making music outside my dining room window. This sound turns my frown into laughter and a big, long smile. I smile for the first time in months. I miss the music of God's creation. I miss smiling at little things that give me joy. I look around me and see my daughter sitting in the mirror, looking hopeless. Then it hits me that I am the cause of this emotion. What am I doing with a big plate of junk food in my hand? Why am I not outside giving my daughter all the opportunities of exploring? I see my reflection in the mirror, and I gasp out of shock. WHAT?! How did I get this big? My emotions let loose. It's like a big thunderstorm of tears. I cry out of anger and out of fear. My daughter runs to me and puts her hands on my face. She picks up my head and makes me look at her. She tells me she loves me by the way she looks at me with her eyes. I look at her with messy hair, baggy clothes and tears running down my face. I say to her, "I am so sorry you feel like you have to help me as a person. It is not your job to fix me, my dear. It's your job to glorify God and to enjoy your childhood." Haven's smile, with those two front teeth, is laced with worry. She runs to me and hugs me. I feel her love and for the first time I don't feel so lost. The dark cloud that once was all around me is now gone. Life looks so bright and beautiful. I feel like a lost sheep that was just found by the good shepherd, Jesus.

I pick up the phone and call my husband. I tell him I feel different and happy. My husband says nothing, but I can hear him tearing up. I tell him I need therapy and I need his help. My husband says, "Welcome back, Erin! I am proud of you for coming out of your depression and realizing that you need help. I will help you get through this storm. Everything will be okay. God will be with you through your healing journey." I hear his words clearly, not like a faint whisper. After I get off the phone, I call a biblical therapist who works in EMDR. When my phone is dialing, my hand is shaking like I had too many cups of coffee. I gasp for air. I have no words to say. Then I hear this calming, happy voice. I feel safe and draw near to the phone. She explains the process of EMDR and how God will work with us during this hard recovery journey. She tells me she is proud of me and thanks me for calling her to get help. She asks me to get a pen and a paper. My nervousness kicks in. I pick up the pen and I drop it three times on the ground. The pen does not work when I start writing. I ask this nice therapist to repeat herself twice. She can hear how afraid I am to schedule this appointment. She pauses and says, "Erin, let's pray, dear."

When she is finished, I can breathe again and focus on what she is saying. Then she starts again by telling me, "Friday at 9:30 am at the San Marcos appointment center." She asks me if I have written those details down and if I could repeat them to her. So I do, and I am proud of myself for not letting my fear get the best of my brain. Then she tells me that she will see me on Friday. I hang up the phone, and I smile. I cannot believe I just asked for help for my postpartum depression. I don't know if I am going to throw up or faint. But by the power of Jesus, I had the strength to call.

If my story relates to you, then this devotional book is the right fit for you. Welcome! This is a book for women who struggle or who are struggling with postpartum depression. This book will help guide you to see the thorns and weeds you need to clean up in your garden. There will be four parts to this devotional book. The first part of this book is called **The Messy Garden**. The second part of this devotional is called **Rich Soil of Truths**, and the third part of this book is called **Planting a Nourishing Flower (You)** and **A Healthy Garden**. Before each section begins, I will have a quote from myself or a Bible verse or from a famous writer. Having quotes, in my opinion, helps the brain to start thinking and helps the reader prepare themselves to be in the mindset to listen and absorb what they're reading. Also, in each section, I will be telling my story and how Postpartum depression affected me. I will be giving you biblical tools to help your mind be in focus on the Lord and to remind you that your depression does not define you. But it's a wake-up call as daughters of the Lord, to see that we have a problem and need help from a pastor, a biblical therapist, and God Himself.

The first section is The **Messy Garden**, where we will discover in our healing journey what healthy items we need to grow our healthy garden. And we will see the cause of the chaos in our lives which makes us colorblind to God's glory all around us. Getting rid of things out of your garden will be hard work and will be messy, but for us to grow a healthy garden, it needs to be done. We can't serve God alone while we hold on to something else that is causing us to lose focus on our Lord. Don't worry ladies, we will have help from a knowledgeable gardener who is Jesus Christ. By God's grace, we will also have God's Word to help us become healthy, planted women who abide in Him. We also will take time to meditate in our journals and write down our trains of thought. Writing down our concept will help us, as ladies, think clearly about how our garden needs to look or will help us rethink how we can improve to grow more beautiful, healthy flowers that shine for Jesus. Cleaning up our personal weeds and thorns will be hard. Telling them they have no more control over us will give us peace. You will see when you let go of these items, that they did not love you back, but were causing you to lose sight of the true Gardener. Yes ladies, this will take time and will probably cause many deep emotions, but believe me sister, God is the only King that will bring you true happiness and true peace in our lives.

The second section will be **Rich Soil of Truths**. In this section, as readers, we will see God's promises and joyful laws for our lives. We will be diving into the love story of Jesus and His ministry. My prayer for you is that while you are reading the Word, you will have your eyes opened to what the Lord wants you to hear and learn. While you read, I kindly suggest that you pray before diving into the holy Word. As a beloved daughter in the Lord, when I open my Bible, I truly believe it's a gift to have the Bible to read. To me the Bible is holy ground because God wrote this book by breathing His words into man. As His people, we should never take for granted His love story for us.

As a Christian writer and daughter of the Lord, I want to grow and share with others about the gospel and how great God is to His people. In Rich Soul of Truths, we also will have a journal time to reflect on what we have learned in each chapter and what key points stood out to us. I think it's important for students to take time to reflect on what God is teaching us and what He wants us to learn. Journal time will help us grow as a Christian in the Lord. We are taking time to meditate, surrender, and be honest (to ourselves and to the Lord). After journal time, I will write down a prayer for you so that you can talk to God. You can come as you are and tell Him anything. He wants a relationship with you. Come today and surrender your burdens at His feet.

The third section will be **Planting A Nourishing Flower (You)**. In this section, because the thorns and the weeds are gone and no longer fogging up our vision, we now can see that we are beautiful, we are loved, and we are important because of Jesus Christ. As daughters of the Lord, we move forward to get ourselves more healthy and planted in the Lord. We see what is right from what is wrong, because we no longer accept these lies of fear. Because our depression is gone, we can see God's freedom of joy, peace, and everlasting love for us. Because of amazing grace, we are no longer women of fear, but new creatures of Jesus Christ. We are no longer defined by our sins or by our depression. But because Jesus sacrificed Himself on the altar (the cross), we are now set completely free! Our gardens are now producing healthy products and beautiful flowers. Let us as God's children rejoice and give thanks to Him for all that He did for us. We can try not because we have to, but because we love the Lord by producing healthy products in our healthy garden. This section, Planting A Nourishing Flower (You), will give you encouraging biblical advice to help you not fall back into your depression and how to keep your eyes focused on God at all times. I will give you resources to heal your postpartum depression by helping you grow in different areas of your emotional trauma: spiritual planting, emotional healing, mental health awareness, improving your well-being, and a heart exam. I will end this section with a journal reflection and prayers to help you meditate on God alone.

The fourth section will be **A Healthy Garden**. At the end of all the chapters, I will send you off with a blessing from myself. I want you to know how much I appreciate you buying and taking time to read my devotional book. I want to send you off with a blessing from God and remind you that you are not alone in this new chapter of your story. We once lost perfect harmony with our Lord and Savior because of the fall, but because of what Jesus did for us on the cross we are now new creatures in the Lord. We can dwell in perfect harmony again with our Gardner. I have a section called Perfect Harmony Once Again, where it's a time to reflect on where you need to grow in the Lord. There will be a contract that you will need to sign. This contract is between you and the Lord. I, as the author, did sign the contract as well. I pray as sisters, we grow, abide, and want to love the Lord with all of our hearts. Making a covenant between the Lord and us will help us become more faithful and committed to becoming a healthy planted woman. After **Perfect Harmony Once Again**, there will be another growth section called **Encouragements For All Healthy Planted Woman**. This section will be a safe area where you can come back and reflect in times of need. I know as a woman, emotions get the best of us sometimes. And in our emotional state, you can turn to these pages and have biblical encouragement to help you have the correct mindset of the Lord. The biblical encouragements will give you the wisdom to choose the Lord instead of fear or depression.

~You will not be alone in this new journey. Also, God is here with you. He is opening your eyes to show you that you need His love and mercy. He is here to help you see more clearly that this depression does not define you, but He does.~
~Erin Broek~

And I pray these pages will help you fight and be strong in your faith. The last portion of the book will be **About the Author**. You can get to know me as a writer and how much I want the gospel to spill over to everyone's hearts. I usually don't like talking about myself because I am a shy person, but knowing about the writer is very helpful.

In closing, child of God, know that you will not be alone through your healing journey. God will be your Lighthouse and will guide you to safety. He is opening your eyes to show you that there is a way to freedom from your depression. Freedom comes from Jesus alone. He is the Way, the Truth, and the Life. Look to Jesus and abide in Him. He will give you rest, His everlasting love and His mercy. Jesus is here to help you see more clearly that your depression does not define you, but only Jesus alone. Sister, I am proud of you and will be praying for you in your healing journey. Be strong, and don't lean back to your depression. Nothing from your past will help you move forward. But keep your eyes focused on God, who will give you freedom from your depression. Take God's hand and let Him guide you through this hard but wonderful new beginning of yours. Let us pray before we start this new journey of cleaning our gardens.

Dear mighty Savior,

I don't know where to start or how I got here. But please, dear Lord, give me the strength to see you clearly. God, I feel so weak and need your everlasting love. Help me get out of my depression. Help me become a healthier person in you. Forgive me when I have been lost in my thoughts, angry with my child, and mad at my husband's joy. God, I want to be how you created me to be. I surrender this depression at your feet, Jesus. Thank you for your help. I love you, great Father!

In your name,

Amen

PART 1 THE MESSY GARDEN

"When Jesus spoke again to the people, he said, "I am the light of the world. Whoever follows me will never walk in darkness but will have the light of life."
~ John 8:12, NIV~

CHAPTER 1 DARK, RAINING CLOUDS

"*L*ife isn't about waiting for the storm to pass. It's about learning how to dance in the rain." ~Vivian Greene~

Feeling emotions as a Christian is allowed. Jesus wants you to come as you are. Please don't tell yourself that you are sinning by having a natural struggle with your emotions. For example, feeling depressed day by day is okay. Being depressed is your body telling you that you are not okay and that you need help. We live in a fallen world instead of perfect unity between the Creator and His people, now sin is crouching at our door holding a grip on us. Beauty is being poisoned by lies of fear in our minds. Yes, Jesus gave us new life, but until Jesus comes back and takes us home, we will struggle through hard emotions. As Christians, we don't want to stay in our emotions. But we need to bring our lament and lay them at the Messiah's feet. Jesus will help us overcome our depression by showing us there is a way to freedom. By abiding in Him and trusting that He is the way, the truth, and the life. Yes, as followers of Christ, we can't just sit around hoping that our depression goes away. We need to clean up our messy garden by taking out the bad weeds and thorns and throwing them away. Our garden won't just appear perfect and healthy by itself. By taking out our negative thorns and unhealthy weeds in our garden, we see that lament brings us to worship God. Not usually at that very moment, but when we come out of the storm, we see how God used our hardship to bring a beautiful story of peace, love, and glory. We also see by the work of the Holy Spirit that we are not defined by our postpartum depression, but we are defined by God alone. Let me tell you a story from my own life where I was struggling with my postpartum depression. By this story, you will see that depression comes in different forms, like social anxiety and panic attacks.

The party began with lots of friends and family. People were loud and even talking over each other because they were so excited to see one another. Not everyone was excited to come to this party. When I entered the house, my heart was beating so fast. I had to tell myself this party was going to be fun and that it was a good idea for me to come. I looked down at my feet making sure I was wearing shoes and was not barefoot. My body was shaking uncontrollably because I am not a social butterfly. I'd rather be at home by myself watching crime shows with my comfortable blanket wrapped around me.

I was faking a smile on my face even though inside I was a nervous wreck. I was thinking, "No one can know how much I am struggling. These ladies won't understand what I am going through." I ended the conversation inside of my head and walked towards the group of women. I still had shaky hands and feet. When the party was done, I got inside of my car. My emotions took over me once again. I felt the deep cloud of depression hovering over my head. I felt like I was drowning in the deep waves of the ocean. This emotion of depression made me cry so hard. Made me cry so hard that both my husband and my child were taken by surprise.

Once again my panic attack started kicking in. I forgot all the training that my therapist had taught me. I felt like I was having a heart attack. But then, something stirred deep inside my heart, I remember that my God was with me. He was using this emotional roller coaster as a learning experience for me. Then little conversations of unanswered questions came into my head for answers. "Will I notice that I am loved by my wonderful family? Will I remember that I am a daughter of the living God?" When these thoughts entered my mind, I came back to reality and I started breathing slowly. Breathing slowly, taking deep breaths to calm my emotions down. I apologized for being emotional to my husband and child. My husband took my hand and started praying out loud. Hearing the words of wisdom put a smile on my face. I smiled at my husband and I knew that everything would be okay. But time would tell when my depression would come back to get the best of me. But in that moment, I whispered to myself that I would abide in God.

~**But in that moment, I whispered to myself that I would abide in God.**~

Have you ever noticed you are having a great time, then all of a sudden, out of nowhere, your emotions hit you like a punch in the gut? You keep telling yourself you are not cursed, but God is using this very moment as a learning opportunity to teach you something. It is easier said than done. While writing this, I am smirking to myself, knowing that I sometimes don't believe that this very moment I am supposed to learn something from my deep thoughts of depression. For example, the root of love is forgiving someone who hurt you, or patience will help you become a better person inside. But in all seriousness, when spiritual welfare comes and attacks us, it is a learning opportunity to see how we will fight in the name of the Lord, how we will armor ourselves in the Word of God. When we are faced with all darkness, will we be strong and say, "In the name of Jesus, I will stand in Him and hold fast in His Word! I will not believe these lies! You will not get the best of me, Satan!"

I pray that we do. We cannot let our emotions win, or listen to the lies that once got the best of Adam and Eve. We don't know at this very moment that God is teaching us how to abide in Him even when we are drowned by the huge waves. We can call out in the name of Jesus. Jesus will grab our hand and will pull us closer to Him. When we are healing and seeing clearly, we can see that Jesus was always around us and He is giving us tools to help strengthen our faith in times of spiritual battles of our minds. We are warriors, women in Christ Jesus. "No one can snatch us out of God's hands" (John 10:28, NIV).

Do you believe that you are a warrior woman in Christ? Do you believe that no one can harm you because Jesus is with you? If not, then I pray that you call out in the name of the Lord. Ask Him to give you strength in your mindset and to give you strength in your walk with Him. So the next time you are scared of entering a room with loads of people or just sitting alone, don't let your emotions win, but remember how Jesus went to the cross out of love for you. He did not want your sins to win, but He wanted to die to overcome death. After Jesus died, death was not the end of the story. Because of the gracious love of Jesus Christ, we now have hope, joy, and everlasting love. We can rely on Him because He knows what we are struggling with. He walked in spiritual welfare but remembered to keep His eyes focused on God alone. When the enemy tried to win, He spoke scripture and did not let fear creep in.

Sisters, let us rejoice to know we are clothed in the righteousness of God, and we are known now for Jesus Christ and not our postpartum depression, our fears, or our anger. We can keep our heads held high. We can smile and take deep breaths because we are free. We once were lost, and now we are daughters of the Lord. Isn't that amazing love? When I remember what Jesus has done for me, I'm at a loss of words. I tear up because I am a messed-up woman who struggles with a messy garden. I tear up because who would want to love me? But Jesus would, and He does. Let us not forget that Jesus cares for us and He loves us with an everlasting love that never runs out.

Ladies, everything will be okay. Do you know why? Because God has our future in His hands. He is shaping everything out right now for us. That means we don't have to worry or fear, but we get to rejoice in the name of the Lord. Relax now, sister. Close your eyes and meditate on these words. Jesus is with you right now. He loves you and wants a personal relationship with you. You don't have to clean yourself up for Him. But run to Him and listen to His words. The next time you are in battle, whisper these words to yourself, "Hush, deep clouds, I am with my Savior right now. You can come in, but I am at peace and no, you cannot rock my boat. You can try, but I know that Jesus will calm you. I will not fear because Jesus is bigger than all of my fears! Fear is a liar, but Jesus is the truth." Let us close in prayer and let us meditate on God Almighty.

Dear Gracious Father,

I need you more than ever. I am scared and don't know what to do. Please help me in this spiritual warfare battle. Give me the strength to fight back in a godly manner. Give me the words to speak. God, I know that you are with me, and I don't have to fear, but I am still scared. Forgive me for letting my emotions get the best of me, dear Lord. Give me peace and understanding. And I know you will, Lord. Thank you for standing with me and fighting my battles beside me. I love you, Lord. You are such an amazing, loving Father. Help me not to forget that. Thank you, Lord.

In your name,

Amen

CHAPTER 2 THE DRY, RED CLAY THAT PRESENTS OUR IDENTITY

"Your mess is a beautiful masterpiece to Jesus."
~Erin Broek~

Have you ever lived in a dry place where the ground is only dry, red clay? When you look at the ground, you think to yourself, "There is no hope for this sad soil." Something is missing from this hard clay. This clay needs nutrients for the soil, lots of watering, and prayer. But for some reason, you are determined to start a beautiful, healthy garden in this dry, red clay. You can see past the faults and start envisioning the beautiful masterpiece that it will have in the end. If you think about this scenario, we are the dry, red clay. Without God, we are dry and dead. We have no purpose or definition. But God doesn't leave us in our destitution. He sees hope in us. He is a gracious, loving Father that wants to help us and give us new life in Him. Like it says in Psalm 34:6 in the NIV, "The poor man called, and the Lord heard him; he saved him out of all his troubles." Like this man, if you cry out to God, He will listen and will help you.

It's hard not to get caught up in our worries, fears, or our anxieties, and not think we are defined by them. But we are not. If those lies are creeping into your head, remind yourself of how God sent His Son to save His people from sin and God's wrath of holiness. Because Jesus was the last sacrificial lamb on the altar, we now have freedom in Christ Jesus. We are defined by Jesus alone. We can look at our dry, red clay faults and not judge ourselves too hard, because we are sinners who are saved by a great Savior, Jesus Christ. We don't have to be ashamed of our gardens. We can stop lying to people about how perfect we are and start showing them how messy we are instead. Our messiness tells a story. Your mess is a beautiful masterpiece to Jesus.

I would not recommend staying in your messy garden but have help from a pastor, EMDR therapist, or a biblical counselor. These wise people are called by God to guide the helpless and the needy. They bring you into God's love story and show you how to use the Bible in your everyday life. They will show you the importance of diving into God's Word by having a personal relationship with Christ. They give you tools to help you fight your depression, fears, or anxiety. You might not see at the moment how these instruments of advice will help you fight away your emotions, but they do, like slow drips of water. Don't be afraid to open up about your struggles and your life. It is not a sin to share how you are feeling or what is hurting you. These people are here to help you see the Light in the darkness. Yes, it will be hard to open up to a stranger, but God is using your story as a testimony to bring others to Christ.

From my personal story, I did seek help from an EMDR therapist, (Eye Movement Desensitization and Reprocessing therapy). I was so guarded and blinded that I could not see a way out of this spiritual warfare battle. I thought I knew what the truth was, but it was rooted in ungodly ways. When I met with my therapist, I was so nervous that I started crying and I wanted to throw up. My therapist reassured me that her office was a safe place. And that, whatever I bring to the table, would not be shared. Hearing these words was like fresh nutrients to my garden. I loved how my therapist's office was painted a calming and welcoming color. She had calming music that was coming from her laptop that sounded like I was relaxing at the beach. Her couch, where I was holding on for dear life, was soft and felt like I was walking on clouds. Her pillows were my shield from hiding my story of hurts. Oils from her diffuser reminded me of the ones I use at my own home. I knew from the moment I walked in that I was safe and that this sweet, welcoming lady was not going to leak out my story to others. But she was going to help me walk in my Christianity story with confidence, joy, and understanding.

Releasing my depression, fears, and my struggles from my past helped me breathe for the first time in months. Because I felt safe opening up, I started losing my grip on the pillows and began smiling and crying at the same time. I knew this lady could help this lost cause. I knew she wasn't going to be my savior and turn my life around completely, but I did know with time, I could see all of that depression that was making me crippled with fear would not have a hold on me anymore. Each time I went, I opened up little by little. I went deeper into the ocean until I was able to go all the way under. Each time I did open up, my therapist told me, "Good job Erin, well done!" For some reason, her saying that was like water for my frail garden that needed help being healthy and planted in biblical wisdom.

When I would walk in the door, I would sit down on her couch. She would first start by asking how I was feeling. She also asked me how my depression affected my week. Did I sit in it, letting it fester in my mind, or did I meditate in God's word? Did I pray and ask for help? I would honestly tell her that I didn't know how to feel, and opening up my Bible scared me. I didn't feel safe when I opened it. I felt like God was judging me for having postpartum depression, and He might strike me down just by feeling this way. By the grace of God, my therapist gently reminded me that we are allowed not to feel okay. It's okay to bring God our hurts and complaints. This statement gave me relief. I had never heard this before. Something in my mind just gave out a loud cry. I felt so relieved and happy knowing my God cared about my hurts. If you are sitting there reading each line thinking to yourself what EMDR therapy does, then let me explain in my own words the best way I can.

My therapist, which I will not name because of my own safety, would ask me to breathe in God's grace and out the fear five times before we began our EMDR session. She would ask me to find a place in my mind where I felt safe. For me, this place was Starbucks. Whenever I felt unsafe or needed to leave just to have my own time I would escape to Starbucks. So I did what she asked. I closed my eyes and thought of myself drinking my iced latte, sitting on the high chairs looking around at everyone coming into the store. I then began breathing more deeply. Then she asked me to come out of my daydream and to look at her. She told me to watch her fingers. Then she took her pointer finger and middle finger and moved them together. I watched the way her two fingers moved back and forth so fast. While I was watching, she asked me to think of the first memory that popped up in my head and hold that memory. Let that memory expand. Why is this memory important to me, or why is this memory making me want to cry?

When my therapist was done moving her fingers, she told me to take a deep breath in and out. From there, I had to share what memory came into my mind. And I had to rate it from 1 to 5, with 5 being the most traumatic memory. Each day I came in, it felt like grabbing my thorns and weeds by the hand and ripping them out of my garden. I knew they had to go, and I could no longer hide from them. They didn't define me, God did. If this method sounds crazy to you or sounds like I am getting hypnotized, let me reassure you that this method is biblical and very helpful to our minds. This tool helped me realize my depression and fear. This tool helped me see the difference between healthy and unhealthy. This tool helped me see that I do have problems that are affecting the way I am as a woman. Fear has a way of affecting the brain, making it believe fear is healthy and that what we see is truth. We all need guidance and help from a wise therapist. We need to make a change and not let our depression or fear let it have a say in our future. We need to break the cycle of our generation. We need not be guarded but have a learning spirit that wants help. Help is not a sign of weakness but the sign of community and growth.

~Help is not the sign of weakness, but the sign of community and growth.~
~Erin Broek~

Dear sisters, if you are contemplating if you need help with your depression, let me be the one to say that you do. Don't walk alone in your depression. If you do, your depression will get harder to handle and will blind you of any joy. Go get help from a pastor, therapist, or a woman at your church that is a counselor. These godly people will help you. But they are not God. And your journey will be hard and won't be done overnight. But with the help of the Holy Spirit, working with these people will help you be free from your depression. Yes, your depression will always be there knocking on your door, but because you asked for help, you are pursuing becoming a healthier woman who will abide in God. If you go and don't like the way a person makes you feel, then it's okay to change and go to someone else. I went to three people before I found the perfect match. Ask God to walk with you in your new story. I know it's hard to see, but God is there planning out your future. Don't lose hope, sister. There is Light in the dark tunnel. You just have to keep walking, keep your eyes focused on God. Let us bring our depression and concerns to our Lord, who hears us when we pray.

Dear merciful Lord,

Thank you for listening to our hurts and our compliments. Thank you for being gracious to us, Lord. You are such a loving, merciful Lord. We are hurt and don't know what to do. We need you to be our Light in our dark tunnel. Lord, asking for help is very hard for us because that shows we are weak and have problems. But we can't do this journey by ourselves, Lord. So please give us courage and understanding to ask for help from a biblical leader. Lord, we don't know what will happen, but we will keep our eyes focused on you. Thank you dear Lord. We love you with all of our hearts.

In your name,

Amen

CHAPTER 3 THE SHARP THORNS THAT NEVER LEAVE OUR SIDE

"Having suffered in your life doesn't mean God doesn't care about you. It means God is working through your hardships to shape you through the storm. When you think deep thoughts remember the cross. The cross shows amazing grace and abundance of love."
~Erin Broek~

Because of what happened between Adam and God, there will always be thorns in our garden. The ground once produced by itself, but because our forefathers disobeyed God's commands, we have to work for our food. But the amazing part of this story in Genesis 3 is that even though Adam and Eve were sent away from the perfect unity of the garden, God clothed them by sacrificing an animal. God never stayed in the garden and closed off communication from His people, but was there for them to help guide them on their new journey in a sinful world. I know when we read the story of the fall, you might think how foolish Adam and Eve were for disobeying God. But when sin creeps in and liars come in with full force, it's hard to put earmuffs on and walk away. Think about if you were there with postpartum depression, and God gave you a rule not to eat the fruit of His tree, and the devil told you that if you ate this fruit, you would be free from postpartum depression. How lovely would that sound to your ears? I know I would think twice and get caught up in that lie and eat the fruit.

The moral of the story, though, is that God forgave His people. Yes, there were consequences, like not having perfect unity with Him, but God never left them alone with sin. God is a Father who is slow to anger and who is an abundance of grace. Doesn't that just make you want to draw Him closer? God is a holy God where sin cannot come into His presence. Before Jesus came, we couldn't worship without a priest on our behalf. But God showed amazing grace and love by sending His Son down to free us from the Holies of Holies. Now we can worship freely in the name of the Lord. God now sees Jesus' perfect righteousness when He sees us. Wow, this statement just takes my breath away. What an amazing Father we have!

~God never stayed in the garden and closed off communication from His people, but was there for them to help guide them on their new journey in a sinful world~
~Erin Broek~

If you are sitting down on your couch or dining room table reading these words and you are thinking, "This might sound nice, but I am a sinner who struggles with depression. I can't bring this to a mighty God!" Dear sister, don't clean yourself up for God. God wants your problems, your fears, and your depression. Give Him your depression. He will show you by His Word how to slowly clean out your garden to produce a healthy one. The Holy Spirit is our counselor to open our eyes to see what God's Word is preaching to our souls. Without Him, we won't understand the Bible. It's like reading one of God's parables that is kind of like a riddle. But praise Jesus that God gave us a helper to counsel us in biblical understanding.

So if you have sharp thorns that have been following you around for so long, lay them at Jesus' feet. Be that woman who falls down cleaning His feet with your tears and your expensive perfume. Don't draw back because you are not perfect by any means or because you are a sinner who is stuck by your thorns. You are not defined by your depression, but you are defined by God alone. When God made you out of His image, He said, "It is very good" (Genesis 1:31, NIV). How amazing to think a holy, perfect God made you and called you very good! Just wow! That puts a joyful and peaceful smile on my face. My Father thinks I am very good. He doesn't say Erin is okay because she struggles with depression. No, He said I am very good because I am created in His likeness.

To have a healthy garden where you are planted in the Lord is, you ask the Lord to guide you in your life. You pray regularly, having a personal relationship with the Lord. Dive into His love story (the Bible). Take time out of your day to meditate on Him. Have alone time away from the tv, the kids, social media, and outside life is what our bodies need. Without God, our souls are dry and in desperate need of everlasting water. Turn on worship music to worship God. Worshiping God is a must, and we need to only worship Him alone. If you are like me that have been hurt by a church or a member of a congregation, please don't stop going to church. God won't hurt you because He is holy and perfect. He will always be a faithful God to you. So please don't stop worshiping Him.

Producing a healthy garden will take time. It is difficult to let go of your past by moving forward in God's everlasting love that will never dry out. You will not be alone gardening your garden. You have the Lord, His Word, and the Holy Spirit working with you to produce that most delightful, warming, and joyous garden anyone has ever seen. Your garden will draw people in who want to hear your story and will want to know how your garden shines so brightly of the Lord. You once were in darkness, but now because of the work of Jesus, you now have a wonderful new story.

I know hearing this is still hard to believe, and you are wishing for this dream, but it's not a dream, but reality. Wake up, sister, and see God is the True gardener that knows how to produce a healthy garden that will never die but will be a place where other people can come and taste and see the wondrous love of Jesus Christ. As I close, my blessing to you is that you will know what is right and true in the midst of spiritual warfare; you will be able to distinguish between what is healthy and what is not, like sharp thorns. I pray that you seek help from the Lord and counselors to help you grow in your spirituality, your mental state, and your physical health. In your growth, I hope you balance your love of God. Without love from God or having a personal relationship with Him, your garden will die. I pray that you will stand true to your faith and not be shaken when your emotions rise high. Lastly, I pray that you stand tall and be firm that the Lord has your future in His hands.

Let us start now by helping our gardens become healthy by praying to our Lord and Savior.

Dear loving Father,

Thank you for giving us the Holy Spirit and giving us your Son, Jesus. Thank you for helping us know we are defined by you and not our depression. Lord, when we are growing our gardens, let us become healthy women in you. Let us distinguish between what is right and wrong. Let us not be turned by liars from the enemy. Lord, we need help and cannot do this without you. Help us grow in you, Lord. We pray that when a big storm comes, we stand firm in abiding in you. Lord, thank you for having our future in your hands. We love you, Lord. Thank you.

In your name,

Amen

CHAPTER 4 A DRIED-OUT FLOWER THAT NEEDS HELP AND GRACE

"Try not to judge people around you. You never know what they are going through. Jesus was kind and tolerant to everyone around Him."
~Erin Broek~

Have you ever seen a flower shriveled up and bent over? You look at this once beautiful flower that just last week was shining marvelously, but because of the lack of nutritious food and devotion, this flower is now past its point of saving. Sadly, we are like that dry flower. It happens when we spend less time with the Lord, yell at our kids, get in our minds too deeply, or get impatient with our husbands. No one is perfect, ladies. Some might act like they have it all together, but no one does. Believe me, when the phone is put down, reality kicks in an reveals an imperfect life. We all need a Savior who can grow us back to life in a healthy and loveable way. Here is my story of how I felt like a dried flower that needed help and grace as a mom and daughter of the Lord.

When you first have a child, you are so excited about being brave as a woman who just gave birth. You tell yourself you cannot believe you just did that. Then reality kicks in when the nurse gets you into a wheelchair and wheels you to your car. She tells you to have a nice day and leaves. You are thinking in your head, "Wait! Where are you going? I am not prepared to grow this little human! Come back and give me the secrets of parenting a child!" Panic starts kicking in, and you are in the backseat with a tiny little human. Your husband is driving 25 miles per hour because Escondido is riddled filled with potholes. Then you get home, and what are you supposed to do now? But little by little, you get the hang of this thing called parenting. Then the hardest part of parenting, in my opinion, is the first two months of your baby's life. You are up all day and all night learning how to nurse, learning how to make a baby stop crying, learning how not to fall asleep while holding a baby at 3:30 in the morning, and learning how to not be depressed. You don't get sleep for the first two months of their life. You are trying to keep a smile on your face and learning how not to get mad because of lack of sleep.

Then something comes in and takes control of your mind and attitude. You were once a smiley, laughing, and loving person who enjoyed life. Now you are this angry, traumatized woman who lives in her house with the shades closed because fear has a grip on you. You keep asking yourself, "How did this happen?" Well, it's called postpartum depression. You have this after you have a traumatizing birth. Everyone tells you giving birth is beautiful and painless, but yours was a bloodbath with lots of complications. You feel ashamed because you don't understand what you did to deserve this war zone so-called giving birth. Because you were so traumatized, you are so angry at your child for putting you in this position; but in reality, your child endured the same traumatizing birth as you. But you still can't even look at them because all you see is that baby who came out covered in blood on your tummy. You cry because you know it's not their fault at all. You feel like a failure as a mother for even thinking those thoughts about your child.

~Because you were so traumatized, you are so angry at your child for putting you in this position, but in reality, your child endured the same traumatizing birth as you.
~Erin Broek~

But praise God that we don't stay in our depression. God was there working with us to teach us a valuable lesson of faithfulness. Even in our depression, God was there. He never left our side. Our spirits just got a little cloudy from depression, making it hard to see if He was even there or just left us drowning in the deep seas. He taught us how to be a mother when we did not have a clue where to begin. He was there sitting with us on that couch when we were all alone in the dark, nursing our babies. He was there protecting our babies from our thoughts and emotions. He was there when we felt like we wanted to give up, but He gave us a persevering spirit to push back the pain and love our child as Christ loves us. God was and still is a faithful Father to us. When God is teaching us in times of hardships, I know it's hard to be taught when life throws you into the sea, but having a learning spirit will help you become a healthier, planted woman who will abide in God. God is giving you the tools to stand firm in Him, so when you do become a dried-out flower who needs help and grace, you will know what to do. I am so thankful that God was with me. I learned so much about praying on my knees that year and learning what it means to cry. Don't lose hope, moms, or believe you are all alone. You are doing what God had planned for you. Remember, you are not a failure, you are not alone, you are not defined by your birth experience, and you are not a dried-out flower. But you are a beautiful mother who is loved by the Creator of the Universe.

Ladies, no one has the perfect birth story. Before the fall, giving birth was meant to be a joyous time of a mother bonding with her child, who she brought into this perfect harmonious world. It was meant to be a beautiful story that shows God's perfect love for His people. But when sin came into the world, now giving birth was a consequence of Eve's disobedience to the Lord. I am not saying that giving birth is not a beautiful moment for a mother and her child, but I am saying that giving birth was supposed to be free from pain and labor. Sadly, we women get Eve's consequences too. But praise the Lord that God doesn't leave us in our pain. He is always there, giving us the tools to help us become the mother He made us to be. With God's help, we can move past our postpartum depression and see how beautiful our child is and be thankful we gave birth. We can now fully love our child and pour it into motherhood because of Jesus's sacrificial love. Because of God's faithfulness, He paints a beautiful picture of what motherhood is meant to look like. So when we are feeling like a dried-up, withered flower, we can call upon the name of the Lord, and we can have joy that God will deliver us by helping us once again become a beautiful flower who shines on its gardener.

If you, as a mom, are still dealing with postpartum depression, then I would gently suggest getting help from a professional who knows how to deal with EMDR. Getting help does seem scary, but what is scary is letting yourself not get better. God created us to be in community with one another. Come into God's community by reaching out for help and grace from a therapist. You will see later in your journey that this was the right call for your mind and for your health. God will be there every step of the way on your new journey of becoming a healthy and planted lady who abides in Him. Let us reach out and call upon the name of the Lord together in prayer. God will listen to us and be there in spirit. Let us pray.

Dear Heavenly Father

We come to you as hopeless women. Motherhood is a big task and we sometimes feel it's just choking us. God, please reach out and save us from these big waves. Lord, forgive us when we forget being a mother is a blessing and not a burden. I am grateful for my child. God, please give us godly wisdom when we are teaching our children. God guides our steps in the different phases of motherhood. We cannot do this without you, Lord. Thank you for never leaving us into the big waves but giving us the perseverance to keep going. We love you so much, Lord. Thank you for your faithfulness, O God. We can see your faithfulness even when our minds are cloudy. Thank you for everything, Lord, even the hardships and our depression.

In your name,

Amen

CHAPTER 5 A WORN, CRACKED BUCKET THAT NEEDS REPAIRS

"Through your brokenness, God is shaping you. Remember to look up to Jesus during the tears and the depression. Hold on, dear Sister. Jesus is not done shaping your future yet. He is guiding you through this storm."
~Erin Broek~

Dear sister,

I know there are lots of days when you feel like a broken, old bucket without purpose. You keep getting hurt by spiritual warfare over and over. You feel like you are being hit by a big wave that is turning you over and over when you are trying to swim to the surface to breathe. But you can't breathe because you are stuck through a repeating cycle. You are asking yourself if you are the only person who is feeling this way. You feel so alone and helpless. Every time you feel good about yourself, then you are hit again by negative thoughts, family problems, and lies about yourself from the devil. You lose hope and become this person who is quiet and dark inside. You don't see yourself getting help or your cracks getting fixed. But one day, you are sitting in church, and the sermon just hits you like a BB gun shooting you right in the stomach. You gasp and look at the pastor. You gasp too loud, and now everyone is looking at you. But your pastor smiles at you and continues preaching.

This was me when I came back to church after being gone for two months. I felt like God sent me to hell. I had everything attack me and felt like there was no hope of rescuing me. I felt like Job in the Bible when every bad event happened to him over and over. But one thing I did fail at, that Job did not, is keeping my eye on God. He was okay with what happened to him. I definitely questioned my faith and talked to God out of anger. Because from the outside, everyone else was having their best year in 2021. People were posting about joyful times with their loved ones. I was at my lowest and couldn't even keep my head up to breathe. But one Sunday, I came back to church. I was sitting down, and my pastor began preaching. He was staring at me, and I felt like he speared me right in the heart. It was a harsh truth I needed to hear. I couldn't keep lying in darkness and depression. I had to get up and get help.

So I let myself be valuable by speaking to the female counselor in our church and telling her what I was going through. She gasped and couldn't believe I had kept that inside and that I was still smiling. I told her that I felt like an old, cracked bucket that needed repairs. I also told her I didn't know what was true and what was a lie. That day I cried for the first time in months. I let someone in and got the love that I needed. That day I told myself that I needed safe boundaries and that I needed help from a therapist. I couldn't walk alone anymore without feeling damaged. I met with my pastor, who sent me to a therapist. He did tell me that this journey would be hard, but if I let myself heal, then you would get better little by little.

Sister, it's not your job to heal yourself. You are not the Holy Spirit. If you try to heal yourself by replacing God, you will get worse. Don't allow yourself to live in fear of not getting help. Getting help is not showing cowardliness, but it's showing boldness in your faith. Getting help from a therapist will be the best gift for you. By going to therapy, you will start seeing the fear slip away little by little and will see that goodness, love, and joy will take their place in your mind and soul. You are opening yourself up to be healed by the One who can heal the sickness and the broken. God wants all your broken parts. Don't hold back. Let Him heal you, dear sister. Please don't hide away and let depression of fear win, but look fear in the face and tell it that it can't have you. Ask God to give you the strength to face your fear and to help you keep looking up to Him.

~Sister, it's not your job to heal yourself. You are not the Holy Spirit.~
~Erin Broek~

As much as we as moms struggle with postpartum depression, if we were not given a child, we wouldn't get to see the blessing that unfolds from God. We wouldn't see our children grow up to be the person that God made them to be. We wouldn't see our child dance to a melody because it just hit the right cord in their body. We wouldn't see our children gasp when they get a present that they have been wanting. We wouldn't see our children come to comfort us when we are at our lost straw. Motherhood is a lot because we are repairing our mental, spiritual, and emotional state. But having a child is God's way of telling us that we need a life-long best friend who will take care of us by bringing joy, laughter, and weirdness into our lives. God knew in our time of despair that we needed a friend who would walk with us but show us how to be okay.

God will give us a new bucket that doesn't have cracks it. And He always has. He gave us new life in Him. He gave us a new mind, a new heart, and new eyes to see that we are loved, we are enough, and we are God's daughters in Him. Yes, the waves will always crash on us and try to pull us into deep waters, but God is there when we cry for help. He is there, grabbing our hands, pulling us closer to Him. He will ask us why we are scared and why we doubt, but those are just answers of love and care. We can know we are great moms because we have a firm foundation in Christ alone. No wave, no depression, and no problems can snatch us out of God's hands. We are permanently in God's family.

We can have confidence that Jesus is coming back soon, coming to get us to be with Him forever and ever. We won't have to stay on this hopeless earth, but someday we will return to the beautiful garden with God forever. There, once again, will be perfect unity because of God and man. There will be no more depression holding us down, no more fear grabbing us, and no more loneliness keeping us from joy. We will finally get to see our loving Father face to face. We will get to enjoy Him by worshiping feely with no sin. How amazing does that sound amazing? It's not a fairytale; it's going to happen, dear sister. So don't lose hope or give up. Rest on God alone, and stay strong in your faith. He will come back and take you home. Let us pray to our wonderful loving Abba!

Dear Abba,

Oh, how wonderful you are! Your daughters cannot wait till you take us home. Sometimes, Lord, it's hard to wait because sin is getting the best of us, Lord. We need help to keep going. Please calm the seas so we stop drowning. Lord, forgive us when we are trying to save ourselves. We need to trust in You and trust that You will heal us. As we wait, Lord, we abide in You. Please come back soon. We love you, Lord.

In your name,

Amen

CHAPTER 6 A KNOWLEDGEABLE BOTANIST THAT OFFERS HELP

"I won't fear because my Jesus doesn't let fear run His life or His ministry. Instead, Jesus lets Scripture be the honey of His soul."
~Erin Broek~

When starting a garden, there is a lot to know about plants and flowers. You need to know what the right soil to buy, the right amount of water, and what kind of vegetation will survive in your area. If you don't have any knowledge about gardening, then you are at a loss. Yes, nowadays, you can watch videos on social media to get help or go to a nursery for plant life. There is a knowledgeable botanist that will offer help to you. You will get more than you asked for because the botanist loves to talk about their profession. You might even have to ask them to stop talking and thank them for helping you understand how to grow a garden. But it's important to have a botanist expert to help you set up your garden in the right way. Without knowing, you will be like me, who kills their garden in the first week.

I told my husband that I wanted to save money and wanted to grow a vegetable garden. We together did research about the right vegetables that would last and grow well in California. We even bought a brand new hose from Costco. I was so excited to produce my own garden and was so excited to eat from it. I went in with a positive attitude and the intention to grow a healthy garden. I went outside, and the last tenant who lived at my house put beautiful garden boxes on each step of every stone step in our backyard. The only problem was these boxes were covered with thorns and weeds. I gasped when I saw this mess. But I was still determined to conquer "the mess" to make a gorgeous garden. I started weeding for an hour. And sadly, I gave up. My hands were bleeding and in pain from pulling and being poked. I told myself I had no idea what I was doing. However, there was one corner of a box that had no weeds or thorns, only beautiful dirt. So I took my seeds and planted them there. I even got out the smelly cow manure soil that helps veggies grow. Lastly, I got out my bucket and watered the seeds and the manure.

I came back the next day and watered the seeds again and again. Nothing was growing despite all my hard work. I got frustrated and was wondering what I did wrong. I found out from my knowledgeable husband that I burnt the seeds with too much cow manure soil and was watering them too much. I laughed but told myself that was not correct. I was going to ask about the internet because the internet never lies. So I typed in my question, and yes, before you say it, my husband was right about my garden problem. He was right that I did not know how to begin growing a garden. Gardening wasn't as fun as I thought, and I quickly learned I was not given a green thumb. But I knew that what this garden needed was a knowledgeable botanist who knew what they were doing.

Our lives are like a garden. We are growing into the people God created us to be. He is growing us with His "seeds," everlasting love, and the healthy soil that will help us bloom. Yes, we have weeds and thorns that will make it hard for us to grow perfectly, but our knowledgeable "botanist," the Lord, will help us clean out what is necessary for our garden to be healthy. When I say healthy, I mean in a godly way. As women in this world today, it's so hard to fight for purity and keep our eyes glued to the Lord. This world has so many expectations for women. But, if we go down that path of wanting to be seen by the world, we will be choked by our thorns and weeds. We will be surrounded by darkness and become self-attention grabbers instead of peacemakers who shine for the love of God.

If we follow Jesus instead of the world, it will be harder to fight for what is right, and we will be persecuted for following Him. I know we live in America, where we won't be burned or hanged, but we still will be shamed and looked down upon because we are Jesus' followers. I pray as Christian women, we take those insults as a compliment because following Jesus will bring us peace and so much relief in our bodies and souls. Jesus will not take from us and leave us with empty hope, but instead will leave us with a beautiful harmony of goodness. Jesus always wants the best for us. His love is free and not the lies of death. Yes, for Jesus, it was costly, but He gave us His everlasting love for free, which shows us how much He truly loves us. He did not have to die for us, but He wanted us to feel what true freedom is. I pray that this statement gives us chills because of its goodness.

~Jesus always wants the best for us. His love is free and not the lies of death. Yes, for Jesus, it was costly, but He gave us His everlasting love for free, which shows us how much He truly loves us.~
~Erin Broek~

When you suffer too long from depression, you lose sight of the love of Jesus and forget about His love story. You know what is true, but it's just washed away by your corrupted, brainwashed, and fearful mind. But Jesus still can reach us through the thick weeds of our garden. He can do miracles in His name. He is an all-powerful Messiah who can heal the hopeless and the lost. He came to save the imperfect people. Even when we feel so lost and so far away from Jesus, we aren't. Jesus is sitting in our garden, helping us remove all our messiness. He is replacing our messiness with a beautiful bunch of pure white lilies. They shine by their Creator because He gently planted them in the correct way with the right amount of loving soil and nutrition. We are those beautiful lilies that have Jesus' handprint on us. When we see ourselves as messy sinners, Jesus sees us as His beautiful creation that rejoice over.

As His beautiful creation, we can rejoice in knowing that we were created by a perfect Savior. He took time to create us and know what was best for us too. Jesus breathed life into us and gave us a name so that we could be known as a symbol of His amazing grace and love. We were created to be helpers for His kingdom. Jesus can even use the weak to lead the strong. So ladies, if you are second-guessing yourself today by thinking you are not ready or you don't have anything to offer others, then you are incorrect. Maybe there are other moms or sisters in Christ that are suffering from traumatic situations that are in need of rescue. Don't wait for someone else to throw a lifeboat to someone in need. Jesus called you to help and to tell your story. Your story will be a testimony of Jesus's amazing love.

Your story might hit home with another woman who needs to hear that someone else has been struggling with depression and fear. Your story might help others see that Jesus is there and is working hard to help them to become a healthy, planted woman who abides in God even when they have weeds and thorns. Your story might help you to see that Jesus is using your garden to help others see the goodness of God. Today ask Jesus to help you have the strength to seek out the hurting and the lost souls. And use your story to help them. You might not have the right words to say, but Jesus will give you the right tools and the right materials to be a helper in Jesus' kingdom. Sisters you have come a long way in your gardens. They once were dry and full of weeds, but they are starting to have beautiful green buds popping up. Take time to rejoice in God's faithfulness and your endurance of hard work. There is still a lot you have to do to make a healthy garden, but don't give up. You have a knowledgeable, gracious botanist who will help you through your journey. Let us thank the Lord for all His help with our garden.

Dear beautiful botanist Creator, Lord, thank you for creating us. Thank you for helping us grow our gardens. You are so patient with us and show us lots of grace. Lord, forget us when we get frustrated or when we get up. God, we cannot grow this garden without you, Lord. Please give us knowledge on how to grow our healthy gardens in Your name. We love you, merciful Savior.

In your name,

Amen

PART 2 RICH SOIL OF TRUTHS

"Do not be anxious about anything, but in everything by prayer and supplication with thanksgiving let your requests be made known to God. And the peace of God, which surpasses all understanding, will guard your hearts and your minds in Christ Jesus." ~Philippians 4:6-7, NIV~

CHAPTER 7 FAITHFUL PLANTER

"Leave your anxiety, fears, and depression at God's feet. Come and draw near to Him. God wants to wash your worries away."
~Erin Broek~

Ladies, now that we know we have a postpartum depression problem, not by choice, of course, but because of the fall in Genesis 3 of the Bible, which resulted in a consequence of painful childbirth. We cannot, as ladies, stay in our depression, but must help ourselves by going outside for a walk and smelling the roses, having morning devotions with our Lord, and using tools from our therapist. These routines are essential to our lives. If we are asking our Lord and Savior to help us but not doing our part by using these tools that the Lord has bestowed on us, then we will not get better. We are not meant to just sit and dwell in our dark thoughts. But we are meant to be healthy women who are planted in God and His Word. We need to let go of our depression and leave it at Jesus' feet. We need to stop thinking we cannot get better, but instead, we need to equip ourselves by knowing we have the endurance to get better thanks to the Holy Spirit. We need to help ourselves by not giving in to our depression but rooting ourselves in daily devotions with the Lord, going monthly to therapy, and cementing ourselves in a godly community at our churches. We are not alone, but we are loved so much by our God, our family, our friends, and by our godly church community.

To give you the story of the fall and why postpartum birth pain was introduced, we have to look at what happened in Genesis 1-3. In Genesis 1, the Trinity creates man and woman. We can see that God is the Creator and not men. He was there before anything. God creates man, but sees that he needs a helper and a partner, so He creates a woman. It's so gracious of God the Creator to give His people responsibilities in the garden. This shows that God cares for His people and that He wants to invite them into His perfect, unified community. God takes His people around their new home and gives them simple instructions that children could follow. God lets Adam and Eve know what not to eat and explains why they should not eat it. Easy right? But sadly, no. The devil comes in and ruins the perfect harmony of God and man in Genesis 3. He tells lies to Eve and makes the forbidden fruit sound better than it actually is. Eve is tempted and gives in. Her eyes are open to sin, and she feels scared and guilty immediately.

Sadly, Adam did not persuade her to dismiss Satan's words.Yes, it was both Adam's and Eve's fault for eating the fruit. Gracious God gives His people a chance to come clean and confess. But, the opportunity sin called blaming comes into play. Instead of taking the fault, Eve blames Satan, and Adam blames God. Wow, what a twist this chapter took. Because Adam and Eve ate the fruit, their eyes were opened to a sinful world. Where perfect harmony between God the Creator and man the creature was, now there was sin. And because of this sin, consequences needed to take place. This is where giving birth comes in. The woman now gets "Intensified labor pains" (Genesis 3:14, CSB). However, God does not leave His people in their shameful sin but sacrifices for them by covering up their nakedness and clothes them in Him. Adam and Eve cannot be in the perfect garden anymore. God tells them to leave. But He still is with them.

In this story of Genesis, which is a real story, we can see sin, love, and saving grace. Even when we blame our Creator, who gave us nothing but love and joy, He still loves us. He does not leave us in our sin but guides us on the path of righteousness to His promised land. Today, we are still in this sinful world that is corrupted by a lack of community, imperfect love, and spiritual warfare. God is still with us on this hopeless planet. As we wait for Jesus to come back and take us to a new earth, we can be assured that God is here to help us build more faithfully in our spirituality mental state, and physical health. God knows that we are struggling and that we need guidance. God is a loving Creator who made men and women like pastors, therapists, and godly family members. God put people in charge by planting a seed in their hearts to counsel people in times of need. That's another glimpse of God's amazing love.

*~Even when we blame our Creator, who gave us nothing but love and joy,
He still loves us. He does not leave us in our sin but guides us on the right
path of righteousness to His promised land.~
~Erin Broek~*

Now we, as God's people, have a chance to grow as healthy women who are planted in God alone and by His love story. Because of what our amazing Gardner did for us in our times of depression, we can seek help without feeling shameful or alone. But we can walk in love and confidence because our God loves us and wants the best for us. The next time we are sitting in our depression and something looks good to our eyes instead of God, we can remember there will be consequences for our actions. We can change our thought processes and remember that God is with us when Satan tells us lies and deceits. We can see the difference between everlasting love and ultimate death.

Ladies, be strong, be faithful, and be wise. We have a mind like Christ. We can see the difference between healthy seeds for our garden, and deadly thorns and weeds that will choke up our production of a well-walled garden. Don't let your depression get the best of your mindset, but remember that we have a knowledgeable Botanist who will be there in all seasons to equip us to become healthy, planted women of God. Don't lose hope or get lost in the weeds, but have perseverance during your depression and fill your garden with godly wisdom and godly joy in the Lord.

I will now leave you with a journal reflection where you can get personal with yourself. This is a time to reflect and be real with yourself about where you need to grow and what things you need to get rid of in your life. Take this time seriously because if you are not real with yourself, then you are fooling yourself, and you won't grow if there is no care. God will give you the right words to say. Don't let this time scare you, but use it as an opportunity for godly growth.

<u>*Journal Reflection:*</u>

1. What is one area in your life that is more pleasing to your eye than God?

____

____

____

____

2. Are you struggling with postpartum depression? If yes, how does postpartum depression make you feel?

____

____

____

____

3. Will you call a pastor or biblical therapist today to get help?

____

____

4. What is one thing you will be taking away from today's devotional?

____

____

____

____

5. In what ways can you grow more in God and less in your deep thoughts of depression?

____

____

____

____

Dear Lord,

First of all, thank you so much for not leaving us in our depression but walking with us to help us get better. Lord, you are so gracious and loving to us. Lord, give us the right tools that we need to get healthy and be equipped with your Word. Lord, forgive us when we are tempted by false fruit. You are the only fruit that is pleasing to our eyes, Lord. We love you so much. In your name,

Amen

CHAPTER 8 ATTENTION TO GARDENING

"Come and sit at Jesus' feet. Listen to His wise words. Don't worry about what you have to get done, but take in the riches of Jesus's law."
~Erin Broek~

Now that we know how to start realizing that we do have postpartum depression and know that getting help will begin to heal us in the correct way, our garden is starting to produce healthy vegetation. We also know that we have access to our knowledgeable Botanist, who will help us in our planting season and will help us become stronger women in His Word. So what is next, you might ask yourself? Well, now it's time to take this godly wisdom and put it into practice in your own life. For example, open God's Word and let this law pour out into your own heart. Call a therapist to schedule an appointment. Go to God's sanctuary on Sundays to freely worship Him. Pray to grow in your relationship with the Lord. Go to women's Bible studies to grow in a godly community. Lastly, help yourself by going on walks and eating healthy. Doing these things will not make you a better Christian, but they will help you see that you need a relationship with the Lord in your soul and that you need help from God to become a healthier Christian.

In Psalm 63, which is my favorite Bible passage, we see that David is letting God know how important He is to him. David longs for God in his life. He is tired and weary, and his soul is dry without God. David knows the importance of worshiping God because it shows God for who He really is. When David is worshiping God, he sees God's glory, power, and everlasting love. God's love for David is the most precious jewel. Glorifying God is the best attribute of David's life. David wants to praise God every day that he is living. David loves how God watches him when he is sleeping, protects him, and is always available to him. Yes, David isn't perfect and even following God He will get persecuted for following God's plan, yet David rejoices in abiding in God. David shines for God in the way he lives his life. He knows God will protect him from evil, so David doesn't worry.

~You, God, are my God, earnestly I seek you, I thirst for you, my whole being longs for you, in a dry and parched land where there is no water.~
~Psalm 63, NIV~

Honesty is a beautiful picture of someone who wants to improve and be the best version of themselves that they can be. They know that they are daughters of the living God. They want to be who God created them to be. I pray for all of us that we don't hide far away from God because of our depression, but we cling to and grow stronger in Him. If we devote ourselves to God and to His Word, we will have love flowing out of our hearts and our mindsets. Yes, fear and depression will creep in and sometimes get the best of us, but we know that God is stronger than our fears and depression. He will be fighting our battles for us. His angel is outside our houses holding a flaming sword to anyone who is against us. Knowing these amazing truths, we don't have to hide away, but instead, we can pour out our hearts to others who are struggling with the same depression. We can praise God when we are at war with our minds. We can see that our souls need God. And that worship is healthier for us than our draining emotions. Resting in God instead of sitting there dwelling in our deep thoughts will free us from our depression.

Sisters, it's easy to be told to act like a character in the Bible, but that's not what we want to do. We want to be like God, who is the main character of the Bible. He is shaping everyone to be more like Him. He is sending them out to the battlefield to spread His love story to the lost souls in the world. He is giving us an opportunity to grow as stronger Christians who abide in Him instead of fearing on the battlefield. We have God and His Word, so we can take out our swords and know that there is nothing that can separate us from the love of God. And we can know that God will be there fighting with us. Knowing these words gives me relief and helps me to breathe fully. It helps me know that everything will be okay because God is on my side. Yes, people can hurt me, and I will have spiritual warfare in my life, but I have the biblical tools to be a healthy, planted woman in God Almighty. I hope these words give you joy and peace. And let your mind be free from that dark cloud that's been hovering above you. Look up, sister. God is changing you to be a warrior woman in Him instead of a fearful woman of depression.

Journal Reflection:

1. Do you hunger for God's presence? What does that look like in your heart?

____

____

____

____

2. Do you let yourself sit in your depression, or do you help yourself out by taking walks, having devotions with God, or going to women's bible studies at church?

____

____

____

____

3. Write down a prayer to God, asking Him to help you with your depression.

____

____

____

____

Dear God,

Thank you for fighting our battles with us. We cannot fight our battles without you. God, thank you for giving us tools to help us become more healthy and planted in Your Word. God, be patient with us when we are healing. We know that You are there, and we see you. Help us always abide in You first. We love you, God.

In your name,

Amen

CHAPTER 9 SLOW PLANTING SEASON

Some days are better than others. We all can defeatist this statement. Some days it seems like we are trapped in a time capsule. We see that everyone is having an amazing year and going for their dreams. But we are still struggling with our depression, sitting on the couch and eating more than we should. We look at ourselves and just feel ashamed. Sometimes we feel like God is the first priority in our lives, and other times, we feel so far away from God. Sometimes we are overjoyed with all the blessings that we have been given from God, and other times we are depressed because we are surrounded by so much spiritual warfare. And sometimes, it's just a slow planting season. Every season is a blessing from God, and we need to be content even in the dark shadows of life.

We see evidence of different seasons of life in the Bible, like in the story of Paul, who was a follower of Christ. He was even one of Jesus' disciples. Paul went around different churches and cities preaching the Gospel to whoever wanted to hear the Word of God. But, some were offended by the way Paul preached in the name of Jesus. In Acts 27:1-28:5, Paul encountered spiritual warfare in His life. He was arrested, got shipwrecked while he was a prisoner, and in spite of getting bitten by a snake, Paul kept preaching and abiding in God. He did not lose hope or give up, but saw this block in the road as an opportunity to be a servant of God to the other prisoners and even the soldiers. Paul gave thanks to the Lord even when he had lost everything. God did bless him by saving the boat from capsizing. God even saved Paul's life by not letting him die from a poisonous snake. Even the soldiers were amazed that Paul didn't die from that bite.

~Every season is a blessing from God, and we need to be content even in the dark shadows of life~
~Erin Broek~

As women who are suffering and have been suffering from post-partum depression, we need to rejoice and give thanks to God. We need to be servants of God to our husbands, children, and even to anyone we come into contact with. Having depression doesn't give us the right to be mean or not gracious. God is letting us go through this postpartum depression so that we can rise up and use this time as an opportunity to be an ambassador of Christ Jesus. We either will become survivors of our hardships and will give back to the women who are suffering and show them amazing grace to the One who knows how we are feeling. Or we can become fearful beings. We will lose sight of Jesus and only see negativity all around us. I pray as daughters of the Lord, we will shake off spiritual warfare when it comes our way and be women who are kind, loving servants and shining of Jesus in our hearts even in the darkest of nights.

Take fear and use it as spiritual growth in your life. Use it as a bright story in your healing process. Let fear be a positive attribute instead of seeing it as your worst nightmare. Don't be offended when things don't go as planned. Maybe God is using this darkness to be the climax of your story. You lament and are sad because we are humans who feel hurt when we are broken, but take your lament as a time to worship the Lord. Come into His presence, ladies. He wants to heal you, He wants to love you, and He wants to give you amazing grace. You letting Jesus take control will help you grow in your messy garden, then you will have a rich soil of truths that will help you produce healthy vegetation. Jesus knows what He is doing, so trust in Him always.

Journal Reflection

1. In hardships, do you usually get angry with God or use it as an opportunity to let yourself grow in the Lord?

____

____

____

____

2. Are you content with the Lord?

____

____

____

____

3. When things don't go your way, how do you react? Are you a servant of God or have you become a monster of fear?

____

____

____

____

4. When is the last time you let your lament turn into worship for Jesus?

____

____

____

____

5. Will you still be a follower of Jesus even if you have spiritual warfare in your life?

____

____

Dear amazing Messiah,

Even in the hard times, we rejoice and give glory to you, Lord. Jesus, thank you for teaching us to lament in times of darkness. We are learning as Christians that we need to trust you even in the slow season of planting. Jesus, sometimes we are weak and cannot even look up, so please give us hope and love. Thank you for never leaving us or forsaking us. We love you so much Lord.

In your name,

Amen

CHAPTER 10 RESTING AT THE BOTANIST'S FEET

"Rest my child. Know I am with you through it all."
~Erin Broek~

I am amazed every time I come into Jesus' presence that I can pray to Him. I am amazed that Jesus hears me when I pray to Him. I am amazed that He takes the time to get to know me and hear my words. I am amazed He wants a personal relationship with me, a sinner. Have you ever thought to yourself why a holy Messiah wants time with a sinner? He didn't come for the perfect people who had it all together, but came for the broken and the messed up people. So when you come into His presence, be real and let Him know what's going on. Lay everything at His feet. If you need to weep at His feet, weep. If you need to get angry at His feet, get angry. If you need to gab at His feet, then gab. If you can't look up, then grab His feet and hold on.

There is no right way to pray, but just come as you are and rest at Jesus' feet. Jesus is our Botanist who is helping us grow our gardens in such a way they are real, healthy, and abiding in Him. Jesus knows about hardships and wants to show us how to live a life that is pleasing to God the Father. But because Jesus knows how to get through this challenging path, He will show us how to have peace in your heart and how to abide in God in the process. Once we learn how to have peace in our hearts and how to abide in Jesus, He will take us to a meadow that has a peaceful river, joyful flowers, and nourishing fresh air where you can breathe in His grace and breathe out the fear and the depression. Even when you see no hope, keep trusting in the knowledgeable Botanist because He will offer help during the provocation path.

~So when you come into His presence, be real and let Him know what's going on. Lay everything at His feet. If you need to weep at His feet, weep. If you need to get angry at His feet, get angry. If you need to gab at His feet, then gab. If you can't look up, then grab His feet and hold on.~
~Erin Broek~

In John 12:1-8, there was a lady who came as she was and cried at Jesus's feet. Not only did she cry, but she also poured her expensive perfume on His feet. She wiped His feet with her hair and even kissed Jesus' feet. How wonderful that Jesus mentioned Mary's name in the Bible. Mary showed her gratitude that she could come into Jesus' presence because she was a woman who was poor. Mary knew Jesus could save her from her sins. Mary knew she had to give Jesus her everything, no matter her reputation or how people were going to judge her. Yes, people did judge her and thought what she did was not okay. Jesus knew what she did was beautiful. He protected her and rebuked people for judging her.

It's a beautiful picture showing how to come as you are as a woman. No matter what your reputation will look like or how you will be judged by people, those things don't matter. Being saved by Jesus, the Messiah, is more important. He is the everlasting water that will never leave us feeling empty or feeling parched. Jesus will help us flourish and grow into beautiful, peaceful flowers that flow with the wind's melodies. Jesus doesn't care how you got to Him; He only cares that you came to Him. Ladies, sit, lay, or cry at the Botanist's feet. You will be freed from your thorns and weeds. You will become loved and planted in nourishing the rich soil of Jesus's truths.

Take some time now to take a deep breath and rejoice, knowing even if you are a sinner or a woman, that you can come to Jesus. Jesus protected women in the Bible and even brought them into His ministry. Jesus never judged women but gave them a new beginning to live in Him. Women knew they could come to Jesus because He was a safe man. Jesus shared the gospel with women and did not see a problem with preaching to a woman. Jesus showed women what true love was meant to be like. Jesus made men see that women are just as equally to them. Jesus loved women and did not look down on them. He never saw them as second-class but as an opportunity to be an instrument for His kingdom. How lovely it is that Jesus doesn't stereotype but loves everyone who comes to Him. We are all created equal in Jesus' eyes. Jesus is enough. Come let us bow down before Jesus and worship Him.

Journal Reflection

1. Do you ever come as you are to Jesus or try to clean yourself up before you come into His presence?

____

____

____

____

2. Do you, as a woman, ever feel like Jesus is judging you because He is a man? Do you know that Jesus is not, and He loves who you are?

____

____

____

____

3. Is there something that you need to give up to Jesus and lay it at His feet?

____

____

____

____

4. Do you know that Jesus can use your story to minister to others who are hurting? If you got the opportunity to share your story to others, would you share it to help people grow in Christ?

____

____

____

____

5. Do you believe that you are free in Christ?

____

____

Dear Jesus,

Thank you that even though I am a woman, I can come into your presence. Jesus, thank you for making me equal in your sight. Jesus, it's so hard being a woman, and I need your help, Lord. I need your love, your strength, and your

understanding. Please hear me when I pray. Thank you for being so gracious and loving toward me. You are an amazing Messiah. I love you, Lord. In your name,

Amen

CHAPTER 11 ENJOYING THE GROWTH OF MY GARDEN

"*Blessed be the God and Father of our Lord Jesus Christ, who according to His abundant mercy has begotten us again to a living hope through the resurrection of Jesus Christ from the dead, to an inheritance incorruptible and undefiled and that does not fade away, reserved in heaven for you, who are kept by the power of God through faith for salvation ready to be revealed in the last time.*"

~1 Peter 1:3-5. NIV~

It's important, as a daughter of the living Lord, to stop and reflect. Reflect on how loving and graceful the Lord was to you. Take time to look around you, and see how God gave you what you needed. You now can see that God is there and that you have a problem. He helped you see more clearly and with more godly wisdom. Your depression now is more manageable. Before, you could barely hold your head up, but now you can breathe in God's grace and have the mindset to breathe out the fear. You now can see that you need to improve your garden by taking out the weeds and the thorns that are causing you grief and blinding you from the truth of God. You now can see that you need to distinguish between what is healthy and what is not. You now can see that you are a messy sinner, but you are a new beautiful creation because of the love of Jesus. Lastly, you now can see that you need to stand true to your faith and not be shaken when your depression is high. You, as a daughter of the Lord, need to stand tall and be firm that the Lord has your future in His hands. God will give us a teachable spirit to balance what is biblical and what is worldly in the midst of spiritual warfare.

In the Bible, we get a glimpse of a man who is in need of healing and saving from his sins. In Matthew 9:1-8, we see a community of friends coming together to bring their paralyzed friend to be saved by Jesus the Messiah. Jesus saw this community of friends have faith that Jesus could heal their friend. Jesus did have compassion for the paralyzed man. Jesus told the man his sins were forgiven. Jesus has the authority to tell someone that they are forgiven, and it is not blasphemy since He truly is the Son of God.

~Reflect on how loving and graceful the Lord was to you. Take time to look around you, and see how God gave you what you needed~
~Erin Broek~

Jesus was there on earth to save the sick and the lost. Jesus also told this crippled man to get up from his mat and walk, and the man did. Because of this shocking miracle, people around this man were filled with amazement and joy. This awe made people praise God and showed that Jesus was truly the Son of God. Sisters, take a moment before God to thank Him for saving you from your depression and giving you a mind that is now healthy and planted in His Word. Be gentle with yourselves. Let your body and mind mediate in the Lord. Don't think deep thoughts or listen to lies, but know God is a gentle Father who is loving towards you and cares for you so much. He is going ahead as your provider.

Sisters, don't forget to see the joy in your healing journey. Look back and see how different you are now since you were pregnant with your child. God helped you raise a human who needed you a hundred percent. This child didn't know how to grow up without your help. God gave you the tools to be that loving mother He created you to be. When you saw no hope in the first year of motherhood, God was shining brightly by laying out your future for you. He gave you the tools that you needed to raise your child in God's sight. He gave you the perseverance that you never thought was possible. There is nothing that Jesus cannot fix, ladies. Our mighty Messiah can save and heal all who come to Him. Don't walk in spiritual darkness, because you will be alone. But walk in the Light, and you will never be alone or forgotten again.

Healing means you are letting go of the broken parts that have been in you far too long. You are taking a stand to say no more. You are opening a new chapter and letting go of the old version of yourself. You are allowing yourself to heal by asking the Holy Spirit to guide you through your healing process. Healing will take time, ladies. It's not overnight. Healing is God's way of letting you rewind and start fresh to guide yourself in a better light in the image of God. So the next time you step in front of the mirror, speak these inspirational words to yourself.

"I am a new and better version of myself because of the love of Jesus. I will not let the past control me anymore because Jesus has already conquered it on the cross. I will walk in the joy of freedom today because I am washed in the blood of Jesus Christ."

Journal Reflection

1. Do you believe Jesus can heal you from your depression?

____

____

____

____

2. Do you reflect and give thanks to the Lord for all that He has done for you?

____

____

____

____

3. Are you grateful that you are a mother?

____

____

____

____

4. Have you apologized to your child for showing them anger and being depressed around them?

____

____

____

____

5. Do you know there is joy in your garden?

____

____

____

____

Dear merciful Messiah,

Thank you for forgiving us of our sins and healing us from our sickness. You are such a gracious Father. We don't deserve to be saved but thank you for saving us. Lord, let us never take the cross for granted. Help us always walk in joy from being free of our sins because of the amazing love you gave us. We love you so much, Lord. Thank you, Thank you, Lord, for everything!

In your name,

Amen

PART 3 PLANTING A NOURISHING FLOWER (YOU)

"Every season is a blessing from God, and we need to be content even in the dark shadows of life."
~Erin Broek~

CHAPTER 12 SPIRITUAL PLANTING

"*L*ove never gives up, never loses faith, is always hopeful, and endures through every circumstance."

~1 Corinthians 13:7~

We all need something to worship in our lives. Sometimes it can be sports, boys, celebrities, authors, movies, children, traveling, or makeup. But I pray what we draw our attention to, and our worship to, is Christ alone. Christ is the only person who will feel our longing hearts. When we worship Jesus, our hearts will be filled with an everlasting love that never leaves us feeling empty, a peace that will give us wisdom in times of battle, and joy that will help us look to Jesus instead of the lies of the devil. Worshiping Jesus is the freedom for our hungry and lost souls. We need Jesus and cannot live without Him. Our gardens will not become healthy without Jesus, the knowledgeable Botanist. Now that we know more about what makes our gardens messy and how to attend to them more graciously let us move more towards how you can see yourself as the nourishing flower God created you to be.

First, do you see yourself as a daughter of the Lord or as a messed-up sinner? If you answered as a messed-up sinner, that is natural.I don't think there is a woman out there that doesn't see herself without blemish. Yes, we are messy sinners who need a Savior. But do you know that we do have a loving, selfless Messiah who has already forgiven you for your sins and now sees you as a beautiful, nourishing flower? How can this be, you might ask, but it's true. Jesus came down to save the lost souls who needed hope and love. He went to the cross to die for our sins once and for all. He took God's wrath for our sins upon Himself and was punished for our consequences. Then Jesus rose again and beat death. Jesus clothed us in His perfect righteousness so now we can come freely into His presence. No longer do we stink of filth, but we are daughters of Jesus. Now when you see yourself as a sinner, you can remind yourself that Jesus has already paid for your sins. (If you want to read more, see Mark 15:37-39). You are forgiven, sister. You can walk in freedom and be filled with the joy of the Lord. You can blossom as a beautiful, healthy flower and people can see that you have a loving Botanist who does take good care of you.

~Worshiping Jesus is the freedom for our hungry and lost souls. We need Jesus and cannot live without Him.~
~Erin Broek~

If you are like me, you know the Word and love Jesus with your whole heart, but you still are having a hard time accepting Jesus's everlasting love into your heart without dirtying it up with guilt and shame. You are not alone in thinking this way. It's easy to read something and believe it, but it's another whole climb up the mountain to let yourself have freedom and grace in your messy heart. But if we want to become healthy women who are planted in biblical truths, then we need to start believing that we are capable of amazing love. We are daughters of the Lord. Guilt and shame are not what we are defined by, but it's just baggage that we have been carrying with us for way too long. It's time to check in our baggage to the Lord and let Him give us a free receipt of an abundance of amazing grace, freedom from guilt and shame, and patience with ourselves in our new journey with Christ.

Instead of staying in complete darkness, we know we are capable of being godly helpers in Christ, and that we can come and sit with Jesus without worrying about fixing ourselves. We can walk with our heads held high instead of staring at the gray sidewalk. We no longer have a reason not to grow in our spiritual walk with the Lord. He has given us the tools to help nourish our garden and watch it bloom. Your garden will still have thorns and weeds in it, but now you have the mindset of Christ that gives you wisdom on what to do and how to take them out. You can rejoice in becoming a knowledgeable botanist yourself. Yes, you will still need guidance from the Lord, but you can have confidence that you know how to grow a healthy garden without killing it with not enough water or too much soil. You will make your garden your own by adding hints of the flavor of the Lord in it. By taking your experiences into your new story, you can start becoming a healthy gardener.

You will see that a garden takes work and patience, but with the right guidance and care, your garden will produce beautiful wisdom. Your garden will be a reflection of God's amazing love for His people. And your garden will scream the glory of God. When people see your nourishing garden, they will want to draw near and want to know the love story of Christ. When they hear the good news of Christ, they will want to worship with you and will want to become a healthy planted woman in Christ too.

Journal Reflection

1. Does your garden have spiritual growth from the Lord?

____

____

____

____

2. Have you checked your baggage yet to the Lord? Or are you still holding on to your guilt and shame for comfort?

____

____

____

____

3. Do you share the good news of the Lord with others who need help? Or are you scared because you think you don't have the right words to say?

____

____

____

____

4. Do you see yourself as a beautiful, nourishing flower of God?

____

____

____

____

5. Do you clean yourself up before you come in the presence of the Lord, or do you come as you are?

———————————————————————————————————

———————————————————————————————————

———————————————————————————————————

Dear Messiah, Thank you for saving us and shaping us into a vessel for your kingdom. Jesus, we confess that sometimes we do listen to the wrong voice. Forgive us when we give into our guilt and shame and not you. Lord, we give you our baggage and surrender them to you. Give us strength not to pick them up again but to leave them at your feet. Thank you for helping us, dear Lord. We love you.

In your name,

Amen

CHAPTER 13 EMOTIONAL HEALING

"Healing means you are letting go of the broken parts that have been on you way too long. You are taking a stance of saying no more."

~Erin Broek~

Emotional healing is one aspect we, as women, should take very seriously. We are like a train that runs on coal, but instead of coal, we run on our emotions. If we don't feel centered, then our train stops and maybe even runs off the train tracks. We start thinking too deeply and maybe even run a scenario in our heads that we might have let our emotions run the train. Sometimes, being a woman is hard because our body is working so much during our menstruation cycle or even when we growing a human inside of us.

As women, we need to ask God to give us godly wisdom and to help us see clearly what He wants us to see. We also need to ask God to give us strength and not rely on our heavy emotions. Having emotions is not wrong to act upon. But having your world center upon your problems, hurts, or fears instead of centering your mind upon God will not help you heal or become a healthy woman who is planted in the Lord.

Sometimes that is where Satan can get the best of us. But God gave us an amazing gift which is His Word, and He gave us His helper, the Holy Spirit. This way, as women of the Lord, we can look through the lenses of Scripture and call upon the name of the Lord to help guide us in our journey. God will show us the right way to follow, and sometimes He will let us make mistakes to show us how important it is to follow Him. Don't listen to Satan's lies, ladies. You are loved by God the Father.

"Having emotions is not wrong to act upon. But having your world center upon your problems, hurts, or fears instead of centering your mind upon God will not help you heal and won't help you become a healthy woman who is planted in the Lord."
~Erin Broek~

Sometimes we will have an instinct or an emotion that will hinder us from making a decision at that very moment, or our emotions will give off a signal telling us to set safe boundaries for ourselves. Having these types of emotions, I think, is from the Lord giving us godly wisdom which helps us distinguish between what is healthy and what is not safe. Our emotions are a powerful tool that can either guide us in profound ways to heal, or can destroy our lives by using them as a weapon to hurt others. As women, we need to understand the emotions that God has given us to help ourselves begin our new story and move on from our past traumas. Then we can help ourselves with the power of the Holy Spirit in times of deep emotions. Let our spirit be quiet in the presence of God. Let us meditate on the Kings of King. Let us ask God to give our hearts peace that passes all understanding.

But if depression and fear creeps into your mind and decide to stay the night, then try out these encouraging tips to help your emotions not take over your mindset.

• Close your eyes and breathe in God's grace and breathe out the fear.

• When a negative thought appears, address it and try to replace it with something tangible and positive.

• Give a good cry and let out all of your emotions.

• Ask for a hug from someone you feel safe and loved by.

• Meditate on God's Word when you are feeling lonely or feeling empty.

• Write down your thoughts and your emotions in a notebook, and once you write them down, lay them at the feet of Jesus.

• Help yourself out by knowing what triggers you. Knowing what frightens, you will help you heal from center situations.

• Help yourself by knowing when your menstrual cycles are coming up. Have an app on your phone, or write it down on your calendar. Let your husbands know or your friends that you are very sensitive right now in your hearts and that they need to be gentle with you.

• Pray and ask God to give you the strength that you don't have right in this very moment.

• Take a bath to soothe your body, or eat your comfort food.

• Then head to bed and know that God will watch over you when you sleep.

Everything will be okay because you are not alone. Remember, ladies, you are not alone in your emotional healing. The Lord will give you the tools to balance what is right and what is true in the midst of fear. Your souls will be refreshed by your Father's love.

Journal Reflection

1. When you have a big decision coming up, do you usually pray to the Lord, or do you rely on your emotions?

____

____

____

____

2. Do you get help from a therapist to help you heal from your past traumas, or do you just try to fix them yourself by shoving your emotions away without allowing yourself to heal?

____

____

____

____

3. . Have you asked God to give you strength in times of deep depression? Or do you let yourself think deep thoughts?

____

____

____

____

4. Do you consider yourself a healthy person or someone who likes being sick because being unhealthy is your comfort zone?

____

____

____

____

5. Do you use your emotions to help yourself heal, or do you use your emotions as a weapon to hurt others?

____

____

____

____

Dear heavenly Father, Lord, when our thoughts get too strong for us, please show us the way we are supposed to follow. Lord, it's so hard to be a woman, but please never let us use our emotions as an excuse not to be healthy women in you. Lord, please give us eyes to see what is right and what is wrong. Thank you for guiding us and making us in your image. You are a wonderful loving Father. We love you.

In Your name,

Amen

CHAPTER 14 MENTAL HEALTH AWARENESS

"I have postpartum depression, and that's okay. Doesn't mean I am a bad mom, just means that I am struggling as a human."

~Erin Broek~

Your mindset is a very powerful tool. Your mind produces endorphins that can give you the joy to persevere through struggles like postpartum depression or give you strength to fight through spiritual warfare. Before the fall of Genesis 3, we had a mindset like Christ; and one like Christ, one that sought no wrongdoing and wanted to perfectly obey God out of love. But sadly, temptation got the best of our mindset, and sin won over godly obedience. Thankfully, because of the love of Jesus, who died on the cross and rose again, we get a mindset once again like Christ. Because we live in a sinful world, we fight hard for purity, obedience to the Lord, and faithfulness in the midst of spiritual warfare. God is with us and even fights our battles alongside us. God's Word is our shining sword that radiates the truth in the darkness of battle.

We need to know, as Christian women, that maintaining our faith is a daily battle. Yes, we will be tempted because we live in a fallen world where sin is all around us. But God won't give us too much that we can't handle. We can cry out in the midst of struggles, and the Lord will give us strength in our mindset. We can use Scripture as a weapon against Satan. We can recite verses in Scripture that will help our minds stay focused on God. We can also use prayer to call upon the name of the Lord. In our deepest darkness of nights, God will protect us and save us from our pits of destruction. "He brought me up out of the pits of destruction out of the mud; and he set my feet on the rock, making my footsteps firm" (Psalm 40:2 NASB). If we have no words and our world seems like it's crashing down all around us, run to Jesus, ladies. Jesus has been through hardships and spiritual warfare. Remember to keep your eyes on God and let the Bible be the song of your heart.

~Ladies, God is with us and even fights our battles with us. God's word is our shining sword that radiates the truth in the darkness of battle~
~Erin Broek~

Everyone, in their due time, needs godly therapy. Therapy will help us grow past our hurts and traumas. Therapy will help you see that you are not defined by your problems or fears. Therapy will give you the tools to heal in a healthy way. If depression has got the best of your mindset, then you need to call and make an appointment to seek help from a therapist. Don't be afraid; therapy is a blessing from God. We do need help from people who have studied how to help others heal from past traumas. Therapists make healing much easier because they understand the brain and how to help people who are lost in their mindset. These therapists saw that their calling was from the Lord, and they wanted to help the weak and the lost in Jesus' name. Their goal is to help people see that they are not defined by their emotions. But that God is stronger, and He will heal the weak and the lost souls.

Yes, as clients, we can go to therapy, but we have a job to do too. We need to give ourselves permission to heal from our past hurts and trauma. We need to pray and ask God to counsel us through our new story. If we don't take the tools from our therapist or don't let God heal us, we won't heal. We will stay stuck in the thorns and the weeds. We will allow our messy garden to take control of us and our story. We will be devoured by the darkness. That's why mental health awareness is crucial. Ladies, we all need a Savior that will pick our broken pieces up and put us back together again. We all need everlasting love. We all need to know we will be okay.

Ladies, let God take the steering wheel. He will take you on mind-blowing adventures that will make you believe He is truly the Son of God. Trust in Him. He knows what He is doing as God. By the way, God is the Creator of the universe. Don't be afraid, sister, in your healing process. Give God your depression. It will make your journey so much easier. God will help you to see there is more to your story than your postpartum depression. Calm your minds tonight. Rest in knowing God has your future in His hands. Now exhale that fear and hold fast to God's promises.

Journal Reflection

1. Have you scheduled an appointment yet to go see a therapist? Or are you just staring at the phone, waiting for a good opportunity to call?

____

____

____

____

2. Have you let temptation rule your mindset, or have you, out of loving obedience, kept your mind clean?

____

____

____

____

3. Do you memorize Scripture to help your mind be devoted to the Lord? Or do you just read the Bible to check off your to-do list?

____

____

____

____

4. Do you know God is fighting in the battle with you? Or does it seem like you are fighting alone?

____

____

____

____

5. Do you trust in God? Or yourself?

____

____

____

____

Dear Lord,

Please help fight this battle with me. I don't have the strength to fight alone. Thank you for never leaving me in the pits of destruction. God, sometimes I let temptation win, and for that, I am sorry. Help me to fight for purity even when it's when it's looked down upon by the world. I want to stay true to you, O Lord. Thank you for being my shield. I love you.

In your name,

Amen

CHAPTER 15 BUILDING A GODLY COMMUNITY

"It's okay to want your alone time, but our souls need godly community."

~Erin Broek~

When you are struggling with postpartum depression, you feel like no one else around you is struggling like you are. You feel alone and scared. Going outside is out of the question because you forgot how to be a polite young lady. You forgot how to laugh, how to communicate in a complete sentence, and forgot to have joy in your eyes. But you tell yourself today is a new day. So you get dressed in your best outfit, and you take down the bun that you had up for months. You go toward the door and start grabbing the doorknob, but reality kicks in. Lies start flooding your head. You start hearing, "You're too messed up!" "You can't do this!" "Why are you making yourself suffer trying to go outside?" Your thoughts win, and you take a step backward. You once again lost the war with your depression. You put your hair up in a messy bun and return to your ragged clothes. You take yourself to that same spot you have been sitting in for months, the couch: Once again, you find yourself staring at an empty, hopeless tv while your child plays by themselves on the ground. "How long will this go on for?" you ask yourself. Then something changes in your mindset. You realize it's okay to want to be alone because of your depression, but God made you to be around a godly community. Your soul starts getting hungry for help and biblical wisdom.

You pray for the first time in six months. For some reason, you snap out of your postpartum depression, and you can now see clearly. You can't believe where your depression has gotten you. But you are not mad at yourself or even disgusted. You remember you just gave birth to a human. You are doing your best, but you need to seek help. God gives you the endurance to put one foot in front of the other. You actually make your feet walk to the car. You breathe slowly and tell yourself you need church.

~You once again lost the war with your depression.~
~ Erin Broek~

You drive to where you worship, and you park your car. Your church looks brighter than you remember. You feel the wind singing God's praises and breathe in the smell of fresh-cut grass. You see people you haven't seen in a while waving at you. You know your depression will not win today. You nervously head to the sanctuary. You know you haven't been to church for a while, and you feel guilt, but you know God still loves you. You are proud of yourself and coming as you are. You walk into the sanctuary; tears rush down your face because you hear in your heart, "Welcome home, my child!" Your worship team plays all your favorite praise music. You've never felt so close to God, and you don't want this to end. This day you know God has created just for you. You are glad you came.

Ladies, if you can relate to this story, then reflect on how far you have come. You know it was a hard journey, but you are glad God took you on it. Because you see where you need to be tweaked. You see where God has molded you as a mother. God was with you every step of the way. There was no moment in your depression where God wasn't guiding you. You see now how blinded you were to believe those lies about yourself and as a mother. But God reminds you this is how you were meant to heal in your story. He reminds you to be gentle with yourself. Now that you see clearly how lost you were in your mindset, you know that you need godly mentoring from ladies who experienced postpartum depression like you. You need to join a Bible study again because you remember God created His people to be in harmony with one another, to glorify Him, and to enjoy Him forever.

You slowly but surely start growing in love with the Lord again. But you are scared you might fall back into your depression and hide away from the world once again. But the Lord reminds you that no one can snatch you out of His hands. You are safe with God and at His sanctuary with these women. Each time you show up to your new Bible study, you see yourself heal and give away your suffering to the Lord. You are no longer this angry, fearful, or stressed person, but now you smile and walk in freedom in Christ. You see, a godly community was the right mixer for your soul.

You know now you won't heal fast, that it will be a slow process, but you won't be alone in your new journey. You recite for comfort Psalm 23:4: "I walk through the darkest valley, I will fear no evil, for you are with me; your rod and your staff, they comfort me." You close your eyes and know you will be okay. You won't go back but will grow into a healthy, planted woman because God has given you a beginning of hope, love, and joy in your new story. You smile to yourself and think, "This is very good!"

Journal Reflection

1. How long have you been suffering from postpartum depression?

____

____

____

____

2. Do you let yourself go outside and see God's creation?

____

____

____

____

3. Have you joined a woman's Bible study yet? If not, is there someone at your church that can help you connect with them?

____

____

____

____

4. Write down a compliment about yourself. (For example: I love that you love helping people in need, Erin).

____

____

____

____

5. Write out Psalm 23:4. Know this can be your prayer to the Lord when you are hurting or stuck in darkness. God will help you.

____

____

Dear God,

Thank you for helping me see I need people around me when I am suffering from my depression. God, please walk with me in my journey. I need your wisdom and love always around me. Be patient with me when I sometimes slip back into my dark mindset. I love you, O Lord.

In your name,

Amen

CHAPTER 16 A HEART EXAM

"*L*ove *is patient and kind; love does not envy or boast; it is not arrogant or rude. It does not insist on its own way; it is not irritable or resentful; it does not rejoice at wrongdoing, but rejoices with the truth." ~1 Corinthians 13:4-8a~*

Remember, ladies, you are a new creation in Christ. Your depression, guilt, and shame have already been paid for on the cross by the blood of your Messiah, Jesus Christ. You once were lost, but now you are found in the beauty of amazing grace. Your heart now rejoices in the goodness of the Lord instead of the darkness of Satan's life. You can get off the couch and head out the door with confidence, knowing you are loved, you are beautiful, and you are safe in Christ Jesus. Your garden is no longer a messy garden that won't produce a healthy abundance of God's glory, but now it's growing so much that you are delighted in how much it resembles a beautiful royal garden. You see that God was good to you and still is. You take a deep breath, rejoice in your heart, and let yourself take in the beauty of the hard work that you and God did in your healing journey. You never thought you would heal and be a joyful person who would shine once again for Jesus Christ.

All around you is the shining sun. You love the vitamin D shining on your face. You feel like God is giving you a big hug and telling you that He loves you. You feel so close to God's presence right now. You start crying because a few months ago, you were sitting in darkness, believing lies that were not true. Now you are feeling joyful, free, and so glorious because you're sounded by the true Light of God. Your heart whispers to you, "You are a child of God." You remember, even on your worst days, God still loves you. God will never stop loving you. You don't have to worry about being messy; God will still be there for you and will forgive you. But, ladies, let us never take God's forgiveness for granted. Let us remember how much love was poured on that cross. Jesus did not have to die for us. But He did not want us to feel God's wrath, and He did not want us to feel alone. Jesus protected us on the cross. That is true love.

~Your garden is no longer a messy garden that won't produce a healthy abundance of God's glory, but now it's growing so much that you are delighted in how much it resembles a beautiful royal garden~
~Erin Broek~

Journal Reflection

1. What is something that you will take away from this devotional?

____

____

____

____

2. Write a message thanking the Lord for helping you through your journey.

____

____

____

____

3. Write out Numbers 6:24-26. And remember, you are not alone, sister.

____

____

____

____

4. Write out these words: "I am proud of myself, I am a daughter of the Lord and I am beautiful in God's sight."

____

____

____

____

5. Do you need to ask God for a new heart exam?

____

____

____

____

Dear God, You are an amazing Father. What a journey we have been on together. Thank you for never leaving me. God, I pray this devotional book will be a blessing to everyone that reads it. God, protect these women who are struggling or who have just gotten out of their depression. Give them peace O Lord. We love you.

In your name,

Amen

PART 4 A HEALTHY GARDEN

"You are enough, you are brave, and Jesus loves you!"

~Erin Broek~

CHAPTER 17 A BLESSING FROM THE AUTHOR

My life is built on God's faithfulness. I don't let fear rule my heart. I abide in God and trust Him in all things." ~Erin Broek~

Dear Reader, First of all, I am proud of you for picking up this devotional book. Knowing you have a problem is one thing. But asking for help is showing your deepest weakness. But know we all need help, ladies. We all need a clean heart. We all need joy, peace, and everlasting love. We all need a Savior who will help us get healthy and planted deep in His Word. Depression is so hard to get out of, and only with the help of the Holy Spirit can we get unstuck. Going on the journey to become healthy and rooted in Biblical wisdom is like getting unstuck from quicksand. You feel fine, but with one bad move, you are sinking. But with the help from Jesus, who understands your pain, you can begin again. He will give you a new story that is filled with laughter, freedom, peace, and an understanding of godly wisdom. Without His help, we will return to our depression. We need Jesus even when sometimes we feel we don't. So ladies, with the wisdom you know now, pick up your head. Walk with confidence knowing you are a daughter of the living God. You are a new creature in Him. Don't look back and listen to those ugly lies, but keep your eyes focused on the one true gardener who will help you have a healthy life. Yes, this process will take time and won't happen overnight. But you will wake up smiling, knowing you are free from depression because of the love of God. May God bless you in this new journey of yours. You are not alone, sister. Look up and smell the beautiful roses that God has created.

Your sister in Christ,

Erin Broek

CHAPTER 18 PERFECT HARMONY ONCE AGAIN

"*The more we meditate in the Word, the more gracious mother and wife we will become.*"

~Erin Broek~

What is one thing you will be taken away from this devotional that you want to change in your life?

____

____

____

____

Will you surrender your weakness to the Lord God? What does asking for help from the Lord look like to you?

____

____

____

____

Now write down a prayer to the Lord, giving thanks to Him for being with you and never leaving you alone.

____

____

____

____

Before you begin your new story, I want you to sign an agreement with yourself and before God. Dear God, I no longer want to be the girl who is defined by fear or depression. I need your help, dear Lord. Give me the strength to say no to my emotions and yes to calling upon your name in times of weakness. I promise to become a healthier Christian, a healthier mom, and a healthier wife. Not because I have to, but because I want to know you better without my sin blinding me, O God. I want to be defined as a healthy, planted woman who abides in you. I am giving you my weakness and my sin. I will not pick them back up again. I lay them at your feet, O God. I love you, sweet loving Father.

Sign here:_______________________________

Date:_______________________________

I will join you on this new journey. Here is my signature:

Erin Cathleen Broek

December 27, 2022

I will leave you with this beautiful message from God's word. "But seek first the kingdom of God and his righteousness, and all these things will be added to you. Therefore do not be anxious about tomorrow, for tomorrow will be anxious for itself. Sufficient for the day is its own trouble." Matthew 6:33-34, NIV

Now that Jesus has given you a new heart, we need to ask God daily to give us a heart exam. We need to make sure our hearts are following Jesus and not worldly things that will fill us up with hopeless truths. But that we stand confidently in Jesus Christ as His daughter. Only Jesus' love will fill our hearts with an everlasting love that will give us that hope that our hearts need. His love will never die or run out. Isn't this amazing news? We can come to Jesus anytime we want. We don't have to hide away our messy hearts, but we can come daily to Jesus, and He will pull us in with amazing grace. He will each day mold us into Himself, showing us how to be godly women in the Word and how to be a servant like Him.

If we come daily to Jesus, we will not feel emptiness in our hearts. We won't feel alone or depressed. But we will feel so much joy that our hearts won't know what to do. It will make us dance like nobody's watching us. Who cares if someone makes fun of us for being a Christian. This should make us not judge but pray for this person. Never be ashamed to be a Christian. Being a Christian is the best gift we can ever receive. So walk with a big smile on your face and let people see Jesus pour out of your heart. Jesus is now giving you a new beginning to your story. It's okay if you mess up and go outside the lines. The story isn't meant to be perfect. Jesus knows we are messy sinners. Our mess is a beautiful portrait of Christ. You learn how to grow and heal from your past mistakes/hurts.

God will be patient with you. Just make sure you let Him in and surrender what you need to so that you can grow into a healthy, planted woman who abides in God. Remember to thank the Lord today for helping you produce a glorious garden that screams His glory. Remember to smile in Jesus's everlasting love. You are free from your depression, ladies. Look to Jesus and abide in Him. I am proud of you, dear sister. You have come a long way. I am tearing up just saying this to you. You have made it. Rest now in Jesus, and He will take care of you. You are not alone. Remember that. God bless you in your new story. Let God take over, and just sit back and see how beautiful His mercies are. "The Lord bless you and keep you; the Lord make his face shine on you and be gracious to you; the Lord turn His face towards you and give you peace" (Numbers 6: 24-26).

CHAPTER 19 ENCOURAGEMENTS FOR A HEALTHY PLANTED WOMAN

Your journey is now beginning. Take time to reflect on everything that the Lord has done for you. Remember, He was there and helped you fight through your postpartum depression. Here are some quotes that I would like to share with you that helped me stay rooted in Christ instead of replying to my emotions. When you see yourself slipping back into the muddy water, come back to these quotes to help you abide in God, the true Gardener.

The good Shepherd helps His people when they are wandering through the wilderness. Jesus gives them hope and brings them back home to the rest of the flocks.________________________

God is truth, not fear.________________________

The Bible is a living Word that can change lives, break addictions, and reveal freedom in Jesus Christ.__________________

Get out of bed each morning with a mindset of being motivated to change. ________________________

Jesus can break addictions and then turn them into a testimony.
____

Be thankful for every circumstance. Even in the biggest storm, Jesus can calm the sea. ______________________________

It's okay to feel anger, but don't linger on it. Sometimes a dance party is the best remedy. ______________________________

When I see a beautiful butterfly fly across the sky, I remember God is always with me, and He always keeps His promises. Then I smile and say, "Thank you, Lord!" Then I take a deep breath in and out. I breathe in God's grace and breathe out the negativity. Then I remember I can do all things because of Jesus Christ!
____

Stop picking up what you just laid down at Jesus' feet. You already asked for forgiveness, and Jesus has already forgiven you.
____

Jesus showed women what love was meant to be like.
____

I remember God is with me always. He will never leave me alone in my fears. ______________________________

Remember to take time with the Lord today. Don't be embarrassed to come before Him. But give Him everything and surrender. The Lord loves you and wants to help you. It's a huge gift that He wants a personal relationship with us. ______________________________

When I was broken, God picked me up and put me back together again. He did not judge me nor scold me. But He showed me amazing grace! ______________________________

Know that you are beautiful just the way you are because God created you out of His own image. ______________________________

When you are facing your biggest fear, just look it in the eyes and say I don't care. You have no grip on me! God is bigger than you. Then leave your fear in God's hands and breathe in God's grace and breathe out your fear. _______________________

Don't doubt Jesus! He is not done writing your story. But have hope because Jesus is on the journey of your story with you! _______________________

Trying something new is wonderful. It is not scary! _______________________

If no one told you today, Jesus loves you! _______________________

The Lord will give you the strength you don't have today! _______________________

Remember your safe words. If you get triggered, remember the tools to help you calm down. Pray out loud to God, and He will help you. Don't let your emotions win today! _______________________

Give thanks to the Lord even when the darkness is all around you! _______________________

Thank you for completing the Story, Jesus! _______________________

"May the God of hope fill you with all joy and peace as you trust in him, so that you may overflow with hope by the power of the Holy Spirit" Romans 15:13, NIV. _______________________

ABOUT THE AUTHOR

"You are God's beautiful poetry to share His love story with others who need love and hope."

~ Erin Broek~

Erin Broek is a Christian author who loves sharing her story with women and men around the world. Erin shares biblical quotes, Bible verses, and messages on her Instagram to help people know that Jesus loves them. Her Instagram is @abideingod.erin. If anyone wants to grow as a healthy planted woman or dive deeper into Jesus's love story. This is Erin's second book that she has written. Her first book is Set Your Compass: A Women's 31 Devotional for Abiding in God, which you can find on Amazon Prime or at Barnes & Noble.

Erin is married to her sweet husband, Spencer Broek. They have been married for three years. They got married when Covid 19 hit. They quickly learned what getting to know someone meant. Through staying home and being trapped, they found that God was their safe place. They had a daughter named Haven which means "safe place". They wanted her to have a name so that she could see God's beautiful wonder of glory. Erin struggled with postpartum depression for six months after having their child. But, by God's grace, she overcame depression. Erin did not want any women who have been struggling or are struggling to feel alone. Postpartum depression is real and very common in lots of women. Learning and experiencing postpartum depression, she felt it in her heart to write a book about her journey. Through this process, Erin saw this was a learning opportunity from the Lord. she now can see that Jesus was there and His love was all around her even when the sun went down. Erin is not an experiment by any means, but she prays that any woman picking up this book will be blessed and changed by the power of Christ. "I sought the Lord, and he answered me and delivered me from all my fears.

Those who look to him are radiant, and their faces shall never be ashamed."
Psalm 34:4-5, NIV

www.ingramcontent.com/pod-product-compliance
Lightning Source LLC
Chambersburg PA
CBHW031330160726
47993CB00002B/609